Breakthrough

Breakthrough
by
Marsha Malone

MountainView
Publishing
and
Treble Heart Books

Breakthrough
Copyright © 2002
By Marsha Malone
All rights reserved.

Cover design:
Copyright 2002 © Lee Emory
All rights reserved.

MountainView Publishing
and
Treble Heart Books
1284 Overlook Dr.
Sierra Vista, AZ 85635-5512

ISBN: 1-928602-89-4

Dedication

This book is dedicated to my loving mother for her constant and steadfast support.

CHAPTER ONE

Μy breath caught in my throat as I approached the double-glass doors of the ominous building. The door opened to a brick wall. Beckoning me to enter, it threatened to change my life forever. I looked back wistfully to the grassy knoll where my family waited.

I wanted to turn back, to return home with them. *Why am I doing this?* I knew what I told myself for several months now. God called me to this sacrifice so that I might experience a more noble good. I opened the door on the right and stepped through the gaping entryway, wearing my best and most colorful dress, a red and white paisley print, under which the starchy crinoline slip swirled as I walked. On my right arm was the black postulant dress I would wear for the next year of my life.

One more furtive glance to the outside and I turned to avoid a confrontation with the brick wall. I saw a mammoth hallway with a series of blond wood doors. The hallway was lit only by the mid-afternoon sun that shone parallel to the windows that lined the right side of the hall. I went to Ave Maria Dorm, about half way down the corridor.

I opened that door, and was greeted by four plain white muslin cubicles that enclosed the bedroom space for four persons. Forty-one of us entered that day, and I presumed four of us would occupy those spaces. *What have you gotten yourself into*?

I entered the cubicle near the window with my name pinned to the curtain. I stood for a moment in the enclosed space, aware that for the moment, I was alone in the room. Suddenly my breath became quite shallow and erratic; my heart raced as I listened to the lively chatter of family and friends who waited outside. I thought I heard Denise and Bob as another family arrived, and I knew I would miss them so much. While everyone outside sounded so excited and happy, I felt apprehensive as though I did not really want to do this.

I carefully set my postulant outfit and bag aside and slowly unbuttoned my dress, slipping it to the floor before I laid it on the white cotton spread that covered my bed for the near future. I put on the underwear worn with the postulant dress. The addition of a plain white tee shirt like my dad and brother wore was a bit strange to me. I covered that with the plain black dress that fell to mid-calf. My white leather pumps must be sent home, so I put on the black cotton stockings and nun's oxfords. A white, circular celluloid collar held together by a small black bow tie completed this part of the outfit.

I searched the small muslin space for a mirror that I might get a glimpse of myself, but found none. I realized my identity was slipping away as I folded my pretty clothes and packed them in the bag to give my family at the end of the entrance ceremony.

I left the cubicle and came face-to-face with another young woman who looked very similar to what I thought I did. Apparently I was so preoccupied with my own dressing that I never even heard her come into her cubicle. We smiled nervously and exchanged names then entered the hall. Thirty-nine women who looked very much alike awaited us. From now on, each of us must be shaped into the image of a professed sister and taught how to think, speak, and walk like a nun.

When we all gathered in the hallway, we formed two lines, in order of seniority, in preparation for a procession across the street to the parish church for the formal welcome into the community. Our families were escorted to the church while we changed our clothing. As we exited the building, the late afternoon sun quickly penetrated the layers of clothing, and I brushed away the sweat that gathered on my brow.

No one spoke as we moved toward the bronze entrance doors of the church. We made this move in silence, thinking of what we were about to do. I really didn't want to think about it, but just to get it over with. Suddenly I was very tired; the emotions spent the last few days of farewell to friends and familiar places drained me more than I realized.

As our silent procession neared the entrance of the church, we heard the sound of the sisters' choir. I knew my sister Lee was in the choir as she was a second-year novice. She and I would live in the same building for the next year. That was a comfort to me. The first two young women reached the last pew in preparation for the walk down the center aisle. I saw some heads turn to get a glimpse of the group, and I searched eagerly for the faces of my family. I saw Mom and Dad almost immediately, half way down the aisle. They looked proper and attentive as they knelt facing the altar. My younger brother and sister, Bob and Denise, turned and faced me, and as my eyes met theirs, I felt tears begin to well up. Quickly, I averted my gaze and turned my glance to the altar; I needed strength now.

I passed their pew as Mom turned toward the aisle. She was crying. Dad sat in his stoic, rigid position, kneeling and facing forward as he reflected his Germanic *never let them know how you feel* countenance, but I knew he was proud and sad all at the same time. We had talked about my going into the convent one day.

"Marsha, I know why you're becoming a nun," he said.

"You do?" I tried to look puzzled.

"Yes," he teased, "you're going because you're afraid you won't find another man like me to marry."

"No, Dad, I'm going because I'm afraid I'll find someone just like you!"

We laughed together and hugged, aware that I was truly my father's daughter who inherited his sense of humor, among other things, including his deep brown eyes. Recalling that memory diverted me and a slight smile crossed my lips at the same second as I noticed my brother Francis, his wife Barbara and their infant Anne. Francis returned the smile as he gently hugged Barbara, who was so fascinated with her little girl.

When at last all of the young ladies in black reached their assigned pews, the ceremony began. I tried to listen and get absorbed in the meaning of the words the provincial was speaking, but they seemed so vague and impersonal. I wondered again about my decision. Was it normal to feel all this confusion right now? Shouldn't I be peaceful and eager to enter this new life? Maybe I could talk with Lee about it later. Maybe she would understand this jumble of emotions, but I didn't want to upset her. *Oh well, I'll play it by ear.*

When the Provincial finished, each of us stepped to the front of the altar to receive the black veil we must wear and learned that we would now be called, "Sister." It was all very simple, certainly, but it would open up a strange new world where personal identity was subordinated to group membership.

The choir began its closing song, and the provincial signaled us to stand, genuflect, and begin our procession through the church and across the street. Now, we were all talk as we awaited the arrival of our families for our final good-byes. Another month must pass before we could see one another again. For the present, everyone hugged and seemed in gay spirits. Of course cameras clicked in abundance. All of us were aware that no pictures were allowed again until after final profession, eight years hence.

The festivities shattered abruptly with the clang of the bell, and we said our final good-byes. Salty tears filled my eyes and washed through the make-up still left from the morning. My neck was becoming raw from the rubbing of the celluloid collar. I turned again for a final look and wave and was overwhelmed with a feeling of sadness and helplessness. I was losing everything I cared about.

Several hours later, I was alone in my cubicle in my floor-length cotton nightgown with long sleeves and high-buttoned neck. The night bell rang, and everyone was supposed to be in bed at its sound. I cracked the curtain just a bit to see the full moon before I climbed into bed, knowing sleep would not come easily. So much happened today and I needed time to reflect in order to make some sense of what I was doing.

I couldn't believe I said good-bye to Mom, Dad, my brothers and sister and other family members, and would not see them for another month. I wanted to call earlier to check on them, to say good-night to Denise and Bob before they went to bed, but phone calls were not allowed except in the case of an emergency until after final profession.

I felt momentarily panic at that realization. Tears welled up and I brushed them away with the edge of the coarse white sheet. Everything looked so colorless and drab here. I hated the lack of color and longed for my room at home. It was vibrant with color, from the rose walls to the multi-flowered spread and the colorful pictures of nature scenes that adorned the walls. Here no pictures adorned the walls, only a crucifix hung above the bed in each cubicle.

Sister John Robert had reminded us at the brief orientation session before we went to bed that the call to this life was a gift from God and required the generosity of each of us to respond. Tonight, it didn't feel like such a gift. I knew it would not be easy making this transition, and I wondered if I was up to the challenge.

As my eyes began to close, I prayed for the grace to be faithful to this call and asked God to help me through the days ahead. Sleep did come, but it was disrupted harshly and violently by the ringing of the rising bell. The door to our room was opened and the sister bell-ringer called aloud, "Lord Jesus preserve us in peace." The two novices who shared the room with the other postulant and I replied, "Amen." And so, the first day of my life began.

CHAPTER TWO

This morning, after a period of meditation, the recitation of the Office of the Blessed Mother in Latin, and Mass, I feared again that I had made a mistake. The Latin prayers and the length of time it all took for prayers was a drag! I didn't know how to meditate, and during that half-hour period I followed my thoughts as they meandered to home, the people I left and the freedom of movement I relinquished. I missed my car, too.

However, in those moments of distracted quiet, I heard myself again saying "Yes," to this call, which was expressed, initially, for me in the words of Isaiah, the prophet of the Old Testament.

"Then I heard the voice of the Lord saying, 'Whom shall we send? Who will go for us?'"

"Here I am," I said, "send me!" (Isaiah 6.8)

I don't know how I knew this, but deep within me was an over-riding sense that I needed to follow this path, although I had no clue at that time that the road would not be straight but would include detours, by-ways and even dead-ends. So be it, I thought.

I was always passionate about life, eager to embrace the challenges it offered. I rarely associated passion with my experience, however. I had been taught that passion was dangerous, bordered on sinful, led to excesses, and needed to be harnessed and controlled. Passion was usually connected with sex and not something a good Catholic girl espoused.

Zeal was an appropriate substitute. It lent an air of holy and sacred to emotional responses to life. Zeal was good; passion was suspect. I determined to be zealous and wanted to do more to build the kingdom of God. I would channel my passion into zeal for service through the vowed life.

That kind of thinking and the prodding of family, priests and nuns I knew brought me here. It felt right to me and I would do my best to follow through. My reverie was interrupted by the sound of the mistress of novices' ring as it gently knocked on the blond wood pew. Now, I hoped, we could go to breakfast. We each went to assigned seats in the large refectory that was lined with rows of dark wooden tables, polished and spotless, but sterile. No plates or silverware sat on the tables, no flowers or centerpieces lent an air of femininity and beauty to the environment.

Last night I learned that each person was assigned a drawer in one of the tables which contained a white place setting and flatware for our meal. The room was bare with the exception of the large crucifix that hung on the center of the front wall. As each of us dragged our stool away from the table and yanked our drawers open to begin arranging our place setting, the room rocked with noise. We were soon reminded by the sound of the mistress of novices' ring on the table to handle things more gently.

Allowed to talk at that meal, our conversations helped to dispel my uneasiness and awkwardness at having a meal with persons whom I didn't yet know. I knew lots of silence would follow in the days to come, but I wasn't ready for it just yet. Any food I ate then would simply lodge in the deep hole created in my gut. I was grateful for this touch of human understanding.

Silence quickly became the norm for most of our waking hours. It was an essential component of this lifestyle. To keep our minds and hearts quiet and still would make us more open and receptive to the voice of God. From the ringing of the night bell at day's end until after morning Mass, we observed what was called "Sacred Silence." There were serious reprimands for anyone who violated that rule. After Mass we could talk to one another, depending on the class of feast day. Some special days and feasts of some saints were observed as first-class feasts. On those days, conversation was allowed at all three meals and throughout the day. We never talked in the sleeping area, unless there was something important to be communicated, and then that was done only in the doorway. On second-class feast days, we could talk at lunch and supper; on third-class feasts, we could talk only at supper. Most of the days were observed as fourth-class feasts, which meant there was no conversation at any meals or throughout the day, except at the designated "recreation" times: 4:00 to 4:30 p.m. and 7:00 to 8:00 p.m.

Life seemed tedious in its routine and the lack of personal initiative and autonomy was very stressful. We did everything in groups, in procession, and in conformity. I recoiled at the realization that this was a continuing process. I would live totally within the confines of the novitiate building or on the road that encircled it, until that day we began college classes across the campus from the novitiate building.

There was not a great distance between those buildings, but it opened up a vast horizon. I could walk the road alone on silence days or with a friend or two on other days. My spirit soared as I entered the college building and heard the sounds of joy and laughter and chatter of other young women who dressed as I had not too many days earlier, and whose lifestyle was much more expansive.

While I could not talk with them, I did smile as I passed them on my way to class, eager to overhear their exploits. Their life seemed so much richer and more diverse than mine just now. Were all this silence and intensity and somberness so necessary for building the kingdom?

On the second Sunday of each month, we visited with our families. That day always evoked such a jumble of emotions. I was eager and happy to anticipate the arrival of Mom, Dad, Denise, John, and Francis and his growing family. Often other relatives came, too. It was wonderful to see them all but exhausting as well. So much talking, it seemed, and so little really said. I longed for the special chats I used to have with Mom alone. There was always a crowd now.

I loved the outings I used to have with Bob and Denise — trips to the beach, or the movies, or the shopping center when I could spoil them with gifts from my pay check. It was always so much fun, and we grew very close. Now, we remained in large classrooms, which we shared with several other families, sitting on student chairs, too big for children and too small for some of my visitors. It was such a formal setting.

The visit lasted three hours, a long time for little children to sit still, and there was always such an air of restraint. I was sure they dreaded that long ride from home and the boring afternoon, but they never let on. I know the promise of supper out on the way home was a bit of an incentive. Everyone asked for Lee who was not able to visit even briefly. I tried to encourage her to be out in the driveway when it was time for the visit to end so everyone could at least see her, but she was pretty inflexible about all of the rules. I dreaded the thought that for the next two years, when they could visit with Lee across the campus every month, I could visit only four times a year. I determined then to find ways to sneak a peak whenever my family was on the campus.

The bell rang to signal the end of the visit, and we began our good-byes. My heart ached as I hugged and kissed them all amidst my tears and theirs. Denise voiced my unspoken question on one of those visits.

"Are you sure you want to stay, Marsha? We'd love to have you back home."

"Yeah, Baby, I'm sure. I just miss you all so much," I sobbed and smiled at the same time. "I'll see you next month. Bye, Bob."

As they exited, turning once again to wave, I regained some control and managed to look happy, I thought. My mom saw through it, I knew, and she would sometimes write to assure me that any time I wanted to come home she and Dad would come for me. I couldn't do that and she knew it, because I had accepted the call to this life. Father McNeill, our parish priest, told Mom one time when she was commenting to him how much she missed Lee and I, "Mrs. Malone, you gave them life, but you don't own them." She never forgot that.

After visiting Sunday, it would be a couple of days before I really invested myself in the activities at hand. I came to welcome the opportunities to grow in the basics of prayer and spirituality. I formed friendships with several of the people with whom I lived, and we shared our concerns and questions about the life we chose to embrace. I thrived in the college scene, and welcomed the opening of my mind to new and exciting information. While the disciplines of religious life were rigorous, the educational experiences enriched and expanded. This helped to connect me to the reasons I came, to love God and serve others as an educator.

When I was confronted with the decision to enter the next phase, to become a novice, I was ready. The determination to pursue religious life was nurtured and strengthened through prayer, and I could do no other.

CHAPTER THREE

When the morning of reception into the novitiate dawned, I was excited and eager to don the habit. It was longer than the postulant dress, and touched the tops of my shoes. I made my own black serge, heavily pleated dress in the previous weeks. I also made the white head gear and guimpe. These were starched by large machines because there were so many of us. In the future, when I lived in a smaller convent, I would starch them by hand. The white veil completed the novice's habit. The latter indicated that I had not yet made vows. The only thing I did not know about was the name I would use for the rest of my life.

Like the other postulants, I submitted three suggestions of names to the Provincial Council, and they would make the determination. It was important, this name change, as it symbolized one more instance of setting aside my previous identity and putting the past behind in order to assume a new life. I did not know if I'd be given any of the names, but hoped that I would at least have a name that I could be proud of.

When the time arrived for the ceremony to begin, we postulants lined up and processed to that same church where we joined the community a year earlier. Families and friends gathered inside as we approached the door. The choir was singing their most joyful hymns. The atmosphere was charged. It was time to make our entrance. I glanced quickly around the church to locate and make contact with loved ones, but this time there was less intensity than the day I left home, one year earlier.

The ceremony was brief. The Provincial explained the significance of the step we were about to take, elaborating on the meaning of the call to religious life and the symbolism of taking the habit and changing our name. We then exited the church so we could don the novice habit and return for the completion of the ceremony.

Lee was assigned to assist me. She was very excited for me and for herself. She was now dressed in the black veil she received that morning in the ceremony where she pronounced vows of poverty, chastity and obedience for three years. Taking the habit involved removing a lock of my hair, which she did gently before placing the coif and veil on my head.

This time, as we entered the church, family and friends gasped audibly. We learned later that they all thought we looked like angels in our habits and white veils. I know we looked quite different.

One at a time we approached the Provincial at the altar steps. I knelt before her, holding my breath. I was greatly relieved when she laid her hands on my head and said, "You will now be known as Sister Mary Francis Anne."

I stood then, feeling quite clumsy and ungainly as I gathered the flowing garment that encircled my shoes and enveloped me in black serge. I was pleased with my name, although it was not my first choice. I wanted some form of Francis, a tribute to my dad, and a symbol of my devotion to St. Francis of Assisi and his love of nature.

When the ceremony was finished, I joined my family and friends in that same classroom where we always met. Lee was there, too. For the next two years, she would visit every month with our family while I would be allowed only four visits per year. She would also move across campus to the building that housed professed sisters in a few days.

Our conversations would now be limited because of the different phases of formation. Professed sisters were not allowed to have conversations with postulants or novices except by special permission, even blood sisters. There was such an air of protectiveness about this call, as though families, friends, or other members of the Order could lead us astray.

I knew some changes would occur as I embarked on this canonical year. The first of those occurred the next morning. I met with Lee after breakfast, and she told me it was necessary to complete the task of shedding my hair. She led me to a cubicle in the large washroom where she helped me remove the veil. I then heard the sound of the razor as it cut away all of my hair. "This will be more comfortable under the veil," she explained. I rubbed my hand over my head and felt a shiver throughout my body. I was able to catch a glimpse of myself in the shiny cubicle door. *Oh, God, I look just like my brother!*

The only studies allowed were theology, the nature and practice of the vows, and the history of the Order and its foundress. It was an intense year and I often felt isolated and introverted. I missed the opportunity of seeing the other students and the walks to and from the college.

The days became long and tedious, punctuated only by occasional breaks in the silence when we gathered in the novitiate room for lecture. There would sometimes be an occasional break in the monotonous recitation of the novice mistress when one of us had a question. The study of the vow of obedience was one that interested me greatly because I wanted assurance that I would not have to relinquish all independent decision making.

Sister John Robert explained the seriousness of that vow. She emphatically stated that we were bound to obey any legitimate command from a superior, as long as it was not sinful. That seemed reasonable since I knew my life was no longer governed by my own desires. From now on I would follow the will of God manifested in the voice of lawful superiors.

As she continued to illustrate her point, I was caught short by what I thought I heard her say. As usual, my face, which was the only part of me visible, reflected my incredulity. That slight movement was captured by her. She looked at me with her penetrating blue eyes.

"Sister Mary Francis Anne, do you have a question about what I said?"

I jumped to my feet, embarrassed to have been discovered and clutched the rosary beads that clung to my side.

"Yes, Sister, I thought you said if the superior told me to water a stick, in virtue of the vow of obedience, I would be required to do it."

She arched her back in a gesture of power and determination and sat upright in her chair, her face reddened as she stared into my face. I shuddered internally, fearful that I would be dismissed from the Order.

"That's correct, Sister. The vow of obedience is serious and essential to religious life."

"I understand that, Sister, but your example doesn't make sense to me."

"If I told you to do that in virtue of the vow, you would have to comply."

The tone of her voice and the rigid posture she now assumed convinced me the discussion on this point was closed. I yielded to the moment and reassured myself that this was strictly hypothetical and would probably not ever happen. It was enough for now to live with the fact that the voice of all superiors, as well as the call of the bell to prayer, meals, recreation, rising and retiring was the voice of God and should be responded to promptly.

Actually, some changes crept into the life. Although we were not allowed to read the newspaper or watch TV during that year, information seeped in that indicated things were changing within and without convent walls. Pope John XXIII opened the doors of the Catholic Church when he announced the convening of the Second Vatican Council. In society at large, significant changes occurred as well. A focus on developing unique personal identity, reconsideration of authority, and personal growth as a priority became part of our own conversations as well.

Many priests and religious sisters and brothers abandoned their commitments and returned to secular life. Some fell in love and chose to marry. Others challenged the hierarchical authority of the Church with regard to its teaching on sexual morality, particularly birth control. The vow of poverty we professed became absurd in light of the emergence of the truly poor who lacked jobs, homes or security of any kind.

Although sheltered from much of this type of discussion during that year, questions and challenges of traditional customs of religious life emerged, even in our little corner of the world. One of the first to go was the practice of Chapter of Faults. Once a week, both groups of novices would gather in our meeting room, turn our chairs to face the back of the room, and one by one proceed to the front of the assembly where we knelt next to the desk of the mistress of novices. We named a fault or misdemeanor that we had committed during the previous week. This was in addition to the requirement of weekly Confession in the Sacrament of Penance. Generally, Chapter was very tedious and boring as sixty novices would announce their fault for the week.

"I broke silence in the hallway."

"I entered another sister's cell."

"I spoke with a professed sister without permission."

One day, I broke the monotony by confessing that I disrupted the silence of the other novices at breakfast.

"I threw a chicken in the crumb bowl and caused the sisters to laugh at a silence meal."

I stood up from the kneeler and returned to my place, unaware that the sister next in line was unable to speak as she was laughing too hard. I noticed others' backs shook, and I heard some snickers as I returned to my place, but I had no idea how many people would be unable to continue.

After Chapter, I knew I needed to approach the novice directress to ask for a penance for disrupting the session. I knelt before her and acknowledged my misdemeanor.

"Well, Sister Mary Francis Anne, we do have to be careful how we describe our faults."

No further penance? Wow, that was worth it. One of the favorite penances for misdemeanors was to untie knots from string saved from packages. This would then be recycled and put to use on future packages. I had spent so many hours at recreation that year untying knots for what I felt were far less disruptive actions. I was surprised and relieved as I stood and exited the room.

I was immediately surrounded by several novices wanting to know what really happened that morning. Sister Martin Marie began.

"I don't know what you did, but I saw this live chicken flying around the crumb bowl. I couldn't stop myself from laughing."

"What did happen, Francis Anne?"

"Last Monday, when I opened the table drawer for breakfast, I saw this small decorative chicken in there. I guess whoever sat there earlier had gotten a small basket from her family for Easter. I reached in, picked the chicken up by the foot, and tossed it into the crumb bowl, which contained the egg shells from breakfast. The chicken landed in the egg shells."

I wasn't deliberately trying to disrupt Chapter of Faults, but I did enjoy the hilarity. We seemed to be much too serious. From then on, others began to lighten the tedious recitation. Within a short time, this practice was discontinued in the professed community and eventually found its way to the novitiate as well.

CHAPTER FOUR

When at last we completed the two years of novitiate, I was relieved and delighted to profess temporary vows as it meant I could leave the "hothouse," as it was called by many, and move across the campus. While I still slept in a muslin cubicle, life offered a few more exciting possibilities. New freedoms now became available; cultural and educational programs in the evenings or on weekends were opened to us as professed members of the religious community. We participated in those events, and I began to feel more like an adult than I had previously.

The study of the vows, spiritual life and theology continued, but the primary focus was on completing academic preparation so that we could be assigned to a province ministry. I was expected to complete a Bachelor of Arts Degree within those next two years. The determination of a major was generally made by the Dean of Students, Sister Mary Solicitas, but there was now some consultation allowed. I was particularly grateful for the intervention of one of the sister faculty members in helping to determine my area of specialization. One day after class, Sister Paulette stopped me.

"Francis Anne, what are you planning to major in while you're here?"

"I've been thinking about math."

"That's absurd," she bellowed. "I like the way you think. Your perceptions of human behavior in groups are astute. You ought to think about majoring in Social Science; you're good at it. Forget math!"

I knew one of her good friends was Sister Juanita, the chair of the math department. As though she sensed my concern at offending her friend, she plowed on.

"I've already told Juanita how I feel. I think you should consider changing. We need good social scientists in the Order."

I was truly flattered by her interest and told her how much I appreciated it.

"Do you think Sister Mary Solicitas will agree?"

"Don't worry about her. If you decide to switch, I'll take it up with her."

When the time came for my appointment with the Dean, I told her of my increased interest in the social sciences and inquired about making sociology my major. I was surprised that I was so forthright, but I knew Sister Paulette had paved the way and that gave me the impetus I needed to speak up for myself.

That was a major turning point for me and I found the classes incredibly interesting. I was excited with the new things I was learning and looked forward to the day when I would teach in one of the high schools of the Order. While I knew first assignments were always to an elementary school, I expected that I would eventually end up in high school. It didn't make too much difference at that point; I was just eager to get out of the rigid and inflexible life style of formation.

As the day for my first missioning began, I was excited and enthusiastic, although a little bit anxious. Lots of rumors circulated about certain convents and superiors who were more or less kind and pleasant. None of us wanted to go to some of the places we heard about. With our closest friends, we talked about our fears and made jokes about being sent to some God-forsaken place.

The Provincial and her Council decided where we went with no input from us. There was an air of secrecy surrounding the announcement of where all one thousand members were assigned for the coming year. At a designated hour, each local superior in every house throughout the province gathered the community together for the reading of the assignments.

I listened very carefully for my name but as the reading went on, I became quite apprehensive. Perhaps the superior skipped my name by mistake. We were almost to the end of the book, I knew. Each convent was listed in alphabetical order, followed by the names of the sisters in seniority, based on date of entrance. My name was the last read. I was going to St. Ulysses Convent in a small farming town to teach at the elementary school there. It was so far. I gulped, apprehensive and concerned about what would lie ahead, as the superior closed the book.

CHAPTER FIVE

As I waited for my parents to arrive to transport me to Peru, Illinois, I felt totally lost. I hoped for a place closer to Chicago where it would be easier to stay in contact with family and friends. All the other sisters in my band stayed in the city. I hoped to live in a smaller convent, too. Five years of institutional living was enough for me. I yearned for a more manageable situation. Enough of bigness!

I knew my parents were disappointed as well, although they didn't say too much. They never wanted to question or challenge for fear they might influence me or make me aware of their preferences. Oh, well, I tried to console myself. This might not be so bad. After all there is something charming about a farm community, I thought, even though I never spent any time in one. I didn't really know anyone in the entire group, except Sister Juanita. I was surely glad that Sister Paulette had smoothed that transition from math to social studies.

We exited the expressway and drove several miles to reach the convent. It was such an old building with lots of doors. I suggested my dad drive to the back as I had my suitcase and a box of books and other personal items to unload. The front entrance was on the second floor of the building and the rear was on the first floor. I suggested they wait in the car until I found someone who could direct us.

I pulled on the worn handle of the heavy wooden door. The opening it created offered the only light in that darkened entryway. As my eyes adjusted to the darkness, I noticed a door open across the hallway and a sister emerged. She was startled to see me but quickly recovered her composure.

"You must be the new faculty member for St. Columbanus. Welcome. We've been expecting you. I'll let Sister Juanita know you're here."

With that, she moved to the far wall in the dim corridor, desperate for a coat of paint, and began to ring a bell in a kind of Morse code: 1-2-1. I called to my parents to come in, and they arrived just as the harsh sound of the bell jarred the late afternoon silence. I was now accustomed to bell ringing; in fact, I had been trained to believe it was the voice of God. Secretly, I doubted the validity of that statement and hoped that in fact, the voice of God was more pleasant.

My parents, however, were startled.

"Does this go on all the time?" Dad asked.

"Will you have one of those bells?" Mom queried.

"Sure will, only since I'm the youngest member here, my number will probably be six-six-six!"

We laughed a bit nervously. While this was totally different from the way we lived at home, it was practical in a house this large to use a bell to signal someone when she had a phone call or a visitor.

An old elevator creaked somewhere down the hall, then the metal door clanged open. Sister Juanita emerged with a flurry and rushed down the darkened hallway toward us.

"Welcome, Sister Mary Francis Anne. We're so happy to have you with us. We've been looking forward to your arrival. How was your trip?" She then turned to my parents.

"It's so good to meet you Mr. and Mrs. Malone. I have heard so many good things about you from some of our sisters. We're pleased to have your daughter with us, and we'll take good care of her."

Her genuine warmth elicited a relieved and grateful smile from Mom and Dad as she continued, "You must be thirsty after the drive. Sister Joseppa, will you please bring some lemonade to Mr. and Mrs. Malone? We'll go up to the parlor on the second floor."

My parents declined because they never adjusted to the rule that prohibited those of us in the Order from eating and drinking with seculars, even family members. We could sit with them, though, but that just seemed so insensitive to them.

"Thanks, Sister, but we'd better be getting home. We've a long drive ahead of us and our two youngest children will be waiting," Dad said.

Mom hugged me, her eyes teary. I knew she didn't find the surroundings that welcoming. The ancient building we entered was five stories tall; three and one half of the floors, I later learned, housed the high school and the remainder was reserved for convent use.

The place was clean, but well used throughout its years, and it was very dingy. Of course, my folks were not allowed to come to the convent area where I would be living, but that would not have done much to dispel their uneasiness about the place.

As Dad said good-bye, he took me by the shoulder and said, "Marsha, you'll be fine. This is all for a reason; I'm sure you will be happy here. We'll see you next month, and I'll just bet you'll feel differently than you do now."

I walked with them to the car and waved them off. I felt forlorn again and lonely. Sister Juanita apparently sensed my sadness, because she scooped up my bag and told me to come upstairs where some other sisters chatted in the community room.

"Not everyone is here right now. In fact, the St. Columbanus faculty is at school getting their classrooms ready for the first day of class. We start earlier here than in Chicago, because we take time off in October so the older students can assist their families with the harvest."

As we approached the elevator, I hesitated, cautious about entrusting myself to its rickety cage. Sister Juanita gently encouraged me to enter the contraption assuring me that it was safe. The creaking continued until we reached the fifth floor and proceeded down the hall to a doorway on the left.

She opened the door and stepped aside so that I might enter. The room was very small, with a dormer ceiling. I crossed the room between the narrow bed and the unadorned dresser to the tiny window. I looked down wistfully to the spot where my parents' car had just been and felt a sudden impulse to cry, but I stifled it for the moment. I turned to look at the rest of the room and consoled myself that it was really the only personal space I would have, and I could make it more comfortable in time. I had some pictures and a few knick-knacks which would soften the drab appearance.

I was delighted when I walked the long block to St. Columbanus School. It was a relatively new structure with large windows and brightly colored halls and classrooms. It cheered me to leave the drab high school convent each morning. The first year went well; the students were eager and cooperative, their parents supportive, and the community of women welcoming and warm. I recalled my dad's words when he left me there and realized that my anxieties at the beginning were unnecessary. I really loved this first assignment and looked forward to another year here.

Unfortunately, when the assignments for the next year came, and we all gathered for the solemn reading, I learned I had been changed to another large institution in Wisconsin, a high school for girls. I expected a difficult change because there was a very strong conservative group of nuns who lived there, and I was apprehensive that the humanizing changes beginning to occur in the Order might not be allowed to surface in Wisconsin.

I consoled myself with the fact that I would have the opportunity to study sociology at the University of Illinois that summer. A number of our sisters studied there during the summer months, so the Order rented a sorority house where we could live in community while we were on this secular campus.

We now wore a modified habit that consisted of a blue mid-calf dress and black veil, which revealed a little of our hair. I enjoyed having my hair again. I never liked having a shaved head, although it was more comfortable under the veil. When we changed to the modified habit, which resembled the postulant dress in many ways, we also returned to our Baptismal names. I was no longer Sister Mary Francis Anne, but once again Sister Marsha.

The questions about changes in religious life floated in all our conversations and those of us at the University speculated about some possible adjustments in our way of life. It was all very exciting, and I had my first major experience with conflict with authority in that summer. The instructor in the demography class assigned each of us a research project we would present to the entire class toward the end of the summer.

My assignment was to design a methodology for population control in India. At that time hearings in the Vatican were being held to discuss the Church's stance on birth control. From what the press reported, there seemed to be a change coming, one that would not take such a definitive stand in opposition to any birth control. As a result, I based much of my presentation on the establishment and implementation of birth control education for residents of India.

I worked hard and was pleased with the quality of the research. The morning I stood before my classmates, in my religious habit, I held the morning paper that bore the headline, *Pope Reaffirms Traditional Teaching on Birth Control.* After we all enjoyed a laugh about the fact that my whole project was based on the impending change, I proceeded with my presentation. I won no points with the Vatican, but the professor felt it was worthy of an *A*.

The summer session ended, and I returned to Peru to begin my packing for the relocation to Wisconsin. I really dreaded this change and was quite apprehensive about how things would go. I shared much of that with Sister Corinne. She was the principal of St. Columbanus and had become a good friend. She drove me the hour and half to my family home so I could meet my mom and dad. They would take me the additional hour and a half to Wisconsin. I was heavy hearted, to say the least.

CHAPTER SIX

I was expected at Miserere Convent before 4:00 p.m. so we transferred my single suitcase to Mom and Dad's car. The Sisters in Peru had given me a plant for my room with a promise to pray for me. Corinne said she would try to visit soon, probably on a three-day weekend when she was free.

Once again, the drive to my assignment was tinged with anxiety and apprehension. We did not make any significant conversation all the way there. I was really preoccupied with what might be waiting for me during my tenure there. Once more I was moving to a large institution. It housed three floors for the high school and a fourth for the convent. There was an elevator, of course, but I seldom found myself taking it. Like the one in Peru, it was old and rather rickety.

One unexpected and joyful surprise was the fact that I would not be living in that large institution but in a small house next door. Three of us had our bedrooms on the second floor with the addition of a small kitchen and living room on the first. There was a full bath on the second floor and a half-bath on the first. It was a much homier alternative, to be sure. We were expected to have our meals and prayers with the community, but when not engaged in those activities or in school events, we enjoyed retreating to our smaller home. I was delighted with that part of the assignment.

The teaching experience was again a positive one. The girls were well-mannered and eager to learn, for the most part. I found the flexibility I was allowed with regard to classroom presentations and structure very delightful. The freshmen required a more traditional classroom style while the seniors enjoyed a more flexible classroom schedule. The junior religion classes were filled with discussion, question and even disagreement. It was a good year academically.

While the three of us who lived in the small house were not particularly close or inclined to spend much time together, I was much more comfortable to return to that space at the end of the day than to remain in the "big house." The larger group consisted of clear "camps" of conservatives and liberals. However, there was definitely more who wanted to hold the line on the way things were than those interested in participating in the changes that began to filter into religious life as a result of the Vatican Council.

To implement these changes, the Provincial and General Councils convened and they began to specify some adaptations for our own community. When the papers arrived from those meetings, I poured over them, reluctant to talk with too many there about my hope and excitement for the future of religious life. Those changes added to my determination to continue in this lifestyle. Perhaps I expected more to come than ever did, but for that moment it was enough to keep me on track.

I needed more intellectual challenge than I received in that group, so I applied and received a National Science Foundation grant to prepare me for high-school sociology teaching. I was nervous when I submitted the paper work to the NSF, thinking they might not be too inclined to accept a member of a religious community. The wait for any word from them seemed interminable, and I feared the length of time indicated the response to my request was negative.

I saw the possibility of this year of study as a way out of the difficult living situation of Miserere Convent. As we learned of the changes in lifestyle promulgated by the Chapters the tensions between the liberals and conservatives mounted. It put all of us on edge because we never knew when to expect an outburst.

If I received the NSF Grant, I would attend classes at the University of Illinois in Chicago. I could return to that area and commute from one of our convents near the campus. My dimming hopes reignited when I received word that I had been one of 24 persons from the country selected for the grant. I raced through the hallway from the mail room and burst into my little house to tell my mates the good news. They were elated for me.

However, when I contacted the Provincial Council with the good news, I was crushed to learn that I could not accept the grant. I was devastated because I feared there would not be another chance for this grant. It also meant that I would likely be reassigned to Miserere for the next year. *The voice of the superior is the Will of God.* I struggled as that message rang through my mind. It seemed absurd not to be able to do this. Think of the money the Order would save on my education; this was an all expenses paid scholarship. How ridiculous. I waited a week or so before I sent my letter indicating I would not be able to accept the grant, but I was not happy with the outcome.

No one ever told me why I couldn't accept the grant and that made me uneasy. Was there something suspicious about my behavior that made the Council unwilling to trust me to study for a year at a secular university? True, some members who began graduate school left religious life upon the completion of their graduate degree. That probably influenced the Council's decision, but I felt betrayed by the system.

I weathered that crisis and looked forward to returning to the campus of the University of Illinois for the second year of my master's program. The community of women who studied there were far more forward in their thinking about the direction of the Order. Their hope and enthusiasm was contagious for me. I imbibed with great joy the possibilities that seemed to be coming. These changes promised to make this a much more attractive life.

That summer, the Provincial Council promulgated a change in dress. It was a fairly benign accommodation. Inside the convent, sisters could remove the habit and veil and wear a simple navy blue skirt and blouse. All of us at Delta Phi Sorority House found the money to make such a purchase of clothing at the local K-Mart. We weren't stylish but we were much more comfortable in those clothes in our non-air-conditioned house in southern Illinois.

The reading of the assignments for the coming year took place during summer school. We gathered according to the regulations and listened for the direction our lives would take for the coming year. I was not surprised to learn that I would return to Miserere. I was pleased to learn I would teach all the sociology courses. That lifted my spirits, but I knew I would not be able to wear the comfortable clothing there. My friends encouraged me to take the lead when I returned or else nothing would change.

I waited several months to don the K-Mart special. As I walked to the varnished door of the refectory, I heard several voices animatedly sharing the day's events. My heart pounded and I wanted to run back to the house and skip supper. But I was here now. I had to take the next step. I was very apprehensive and placed my hand on the knob gingerly and withdrew it almost instantly. This was important, it seemed at that moment. I was helping to introduce the changes that so many there had not even been exposed to. My clothes were simple, navy and inexpensive.

As I turned the knob of the refectory door, my knee banged against it, making a loud noise. As the door opened, several sisters turned their heads to see what had happened. When I entered the room, there was absolute silence. As I proceeded down the main aisle to my seat, I saw the heads of some turn from me as though they looked at something obscene. Several smiled and said hello. Only one person welcomed me to sit down, and she commented on how nice I looked. The food struggled to leave my throat, and I rushed out the door as soon as I could. I felt humiliated and angry. No one said anything more to me that evening, not even my house mates. From that time on, several sisters refused to speak to me, even when I was wearing the habit. The dissension was tearing me up inside and disrupting my effectiveness in the classroom. I feared if I didn't make some changes, I might not profess final vows. I would not live like this.

I contacted the member of the Provincial Council responsible for high school ministry and arranged to meet her in Chicago in ten days. The drive gave me an opportunity to think through my strategy and organize my thoughts. I was once again experiencing panic. I knew how important it was for me to receive permission for a change in residence. Once again, I was unhappy with the lifestyle. *Well, maybe it's about time you faced this, Marsha. It seems like you are less happy than you ever have been and you are often in the midst of conflict. Maybe you ought to leave at the end of the school year.* That was frightening to me. There was this call thing and God would be displeased. I couldn't just give up.

I rang the bell and peered through the glass panels into the empty reception area. It was Saturday. Within a few minutes, I saw Sister Ignacio rushing toward the door. She was a large woman and she still wore the traditional habit, which made me a little uneasy. I didn't know her well enough to know how significant that habit choice was for her. Many sisters wore it as a statement about their views on the changes in religious life.

"Good morning, Sister Marsha. How was your trip? It seems like a pleasant day," she said as she took my arm and led me to the small parlor next door.

"The drive was fine, thanks. This is a good time to travel the toll road. There was almost no traffic until I reached the Illinois-Wisconsin border."

We looked at each other as an uneasy silence permeated the atmosphere. She ruffled her rosary beads and shuffled her feet. I was extremely agitated but tried to maintain composure. I was nervous enough to cry, but I kept my emotions under control.

"Well, Sister, I have your request to move from the high school convent. It is unusual to allow a sister to live away from her place of ministry and the Council would prefer you stay at Miserere. You might be able to bring the others around if you stayed a bit longer. Perhaps it would help if you wore your secular clothes in your house and not to meals. How do you think that would work?"

"Not well, Sister. Many of the sisters I know in Chicago are wearing casual clothes in the convent. Some have even begun to wear them outside the convent, as well."

She interrupted briskly, "Those sisters are outside the intent of the regulation. They have no authority to do such a thing."

She was so indignant I wondered how she felt about the regulation at all. Perhaps she was one of those who opposed any of the new changes.

"I'm not suggesting anything beyond what the rule allows. I am deeply hurt by the attitudes of the very sisters to whom I have been generous in sharing my time, driving to appointments and assisting with their housekeeping chores. It's very painful for me to live like this."

"I'm sure it is, Sister, as you are a kind and compassionate person. Try to understand where they are coming from. Perhaps if you stayed longer and talked with them about the change, you would find them softening some. That is what the Council would prefer."

I made no effort to respond during the silence that followed. I hoped she would continue. I did not want to confront the consequences of a decision that would force me to remain in that living situation. I was adamant about that. Reluctantly, she continued, "However, if you find that intolerable I will bring your request to the Council Meeting next Thursday."

"I would be grateful for that. I have already spoken with the two sisters at St. Patrick and they are very anxious to have a third member. As you know, Sister Patricia Maria will be leaving the Order at Christmas time." In fact, the superior at St. Patrick had already confided in me her uneasiness in living with only one sister for fear people might label them as gay. She felt Sister Generosa appeared a bit masculine and people might get the wrong impression about the two of them. I said nothing about this to Sister Ignacio, of course.

When the letter arrived ten days later, I eagerly opened it and learned my request had been approved, despite the preference of the Council. I was elated and made the necessary arrangements for the move. My chest was considerably lighter and my feet flew across the tile floor as I searched for boxes to begin packing. I moved the next Saturday and on the following Monday walked to the bus stop for my commute to Miserere.

I loved the commute and welcomed the opportunity to participate in a more normal life. This was what most people did to make ends meet. It was what I did to bridge the gaps in my life. My commute was a symbol of my journey.

CHAPTER SEVEN

I was filled with enthusiasm when that year ended, and I moved to Chicago where I would study Sociology as a result of the National Science Foundation Grant. This time I had been given approval by the Council to accept the Grant. I was assigned to live in a convent in the Black Community, an easy commute to the campus of Illinois Institute of Technology. It promised to be an exciting summer.

The Grant provided for a five-week orientation, which allowed the recipients to become acquainted with one another as well as the course of study for the academic year. I was eager to continue and looked forward to knowing many of the people who would study with me. We were a diverse group, men and women, young and middle-aged, married, single, and members of religious communities.

This orientation was followed by the renewal program to prepare us for the profession of final vows. The original band of forty-one had diminished to eight, due to departures through the years. Now a firmly committed group and convinced we would continue in this life for the rest of our lives, we discussed the struggles each of us had weathered while on mission those three years. We were zealous for the work of the Church, the work of the kingdom.

Each of us identified a motto that would guide us during our vowed life, one which reflected some special devotion or phrase that was meaningful to us. That motto would be engraved into the rings we received as Brides of Christ. I spent considerable time in prayer and reflection about what I wanted that inscription to be. I chose "reverence for life." When I submitted it to the Provincial Council, they rejected it because it was not spiritual enough! I was devoted to St. Francis, and I loved life in all its dimensions. Jesus came to give life; why was this not holy enough?

So, my ring contained no motto because I would not sway from my conviction. "My Jesus, mercy," "All for Jesus through Mary," "My Lord and My God," and similar ones did nothing for me. I was guided by "reverence for life" regardless of whether it was engraved in my ring or not.

The Final Profession Ritual was powerful and joyful. I was now on my way to the rest of my life, which included returning for the NSF program and preparation to teach in one of our community high schools, hopefully not back to Miserere! By now, each of us expressed a preference for our ministry in dialogue with the persons involved in that ministry. When there was an agreement between both parties, this was communicated to the Provincial and she and her Council would usually ratify it, unless there were some extenuating circumstances. I was delighted to be returning to the high school from which I graduated, just blocks from my family's home. I knew many of the faculty members there and would live with some of them apart from the institution. That was exciting—to live in an apartment or house away from the school. Apparently, I broke new ground when I moved from Miserere, and it became commonplace within a very short time.

None of that happened, however, as God seemed to have other plans for me. I had been elected to the Provincial Chapter that would choose the leadership for the next three years. I was thrilled to serve as a delegate and privileged to be participating in this new election process. Up to now, leaders were designated by the General Council and Province members had no say in the process. Now, there was an election, although it was not too well organized. We were new at this.

The procedure selected was to allow nominations for each role from the floor and then a vote by the entire assembly. We learned these elections were of the Spirit, but there was no lack of political maneuvering among the delegates to help the Spirit along. I was floored and terrified when my name was placed in nomination for the role of Secretary Provincial. I wanted to teach at Montini High School and return to the West Side and reconnect with friends. I tried to protest, but the delegates prevailed. "The Holy Spirit calls Sister Marsha Malone to serve as Provincial Secretary for three years."

My face felt flushed. I was baffled by this turn of events. Why couldn't my path be a straight one? I loved sociology and groups and teaching. What would I do with this job? Several sisters rushed to me after the election was completed. They were very enthusiastic. This was a new time in religious life and many thought the pace of the Order in implementing some of the changes too slow. I was a relative newcomer, though, and a neophyte in religious life. They simply dismissed my concerns.

I undertook the challenge with prayer and determination. The challenges and opportunities I faced enabled me to find my niche in that role. I made immediate changes in the traditional role, with the assistance of the other leadership members. The function of record-keeper was delegated to another person and the minutes of meetings were taken by a young woman whom I hired.

I grew to love the role as it evolved, not realizing how beneficial my training in sociology would be. I visited every house of the convent, covering three states, that first year. My purpose was simply to meet with each group, listen to their concerns and struggles, and facilitate their disagreements. I was not seen as a threat to the groups but as an asset. I was in their home for them and most seemed to appreciate that.

As the months wore on, I became a bit depressed because of all the stresses I encountered. Visible differences in dress reflected philosophical and spiritual variations as well. Regimented and structured forms were no longer tolerable to many while others languished as the forms disintegrated. The very identity that many came to religious life to claim blurred. Some cried as they lamented the loss of that sense of who they were. Many of the complaints became repetitious.

"I knew who I was when I dressed like a nun, talked like a nun, and walked like a nun."

"How do I know what God wants me to do if I don't hear it from the Provincial?"

"Are we all just supposed to do whatever we want regardless of the needs of the Order?"

Every new change seemed to heighten the tensions and animosity. The General Chapter, the governing and decision-making body for the Order throughout the entire country, announced that sisters would have the option of wearing secular clothes at all times. Those who wanted to retain the traditional habit would have that option as well. This change brought jubilation and it brought agitation.

"Why don't the sisters want to look like sisters? What are they doing that they need to appear anonymous?"

"I don't understand why they don't want to be called 'Sister' any more. I've heard some say 'My name is Elizabeth' or even 'Betty.'"

Gradually, my enthusiasm and zeal wore thin. I knew I couldn't make people feel better about their discomfort. Some even raised questions about the viability of religious life for the future. Perhaps it had run its course. Maybe we were the last generation of women who would commit to a vowed life in community in service to the Church and the Gospel.

I felt swallowed up in the fear, anger, anxiety, depression, and unhappiness I heard in those meetings. It began to chip away at my zest and enthusiasm for the religious life. Fortunately, a gifted spiritual director helped redirect and refocus my energies. With his support and guidance, I was drawn into a recommitment to the call of God in my life.

So it was that I found myself elected to a second three-year term on the leadership team, this time as Assistant Provincial.

CHAPTER EIGHT

I prayed every day that the woman who was Provincial would continue to be healthy and viable. I never felt adequate for the primary leadership role. Fortunately, she was a healthy, holy and amiable woman with whom to collaborate, as were the other women elected to complete the leadership team.

I continued to assume primary responsibility for community life throughout the province. While I did not undertake another safari throughout the region, I became a resource to those communities where persons struggled to deepen the bonds that connected them through improved communication skills. The conflicts and tensions that existed in many of the local communities drained my resources, but I prayed for guidance and courage to do this work to which I had been called.

In addition to the concerns of the community members, I began to develop a set of goals for myself regarding our experiences of religious life. Moving through the various convents, I was painfully aware that the diminished number of sisters left large buildings virtually empty. Some of these convents originally accommodated twenty or more sisters, and now housed only three or four people. It seemed such a waste to maintain so large a residence for so few in light of the growing needs of other members of the area who lacked adequate shelter. The convents could easily be adapted to housing for elderly people who lived in unsafe conditions.

I was apprehensive about bringing this to the other members of the leadership team, because I knew I would stir up an emotional cauldron among our sisters in those large convents. However, I was pleasantly surprised when my request to pursue some course of action regarding the redistribution of resources was given support by the Council.

I was aware of two such convents only a few miles apart and grossly underutilized. The local parish convents tied in significantly to the pastors of the parishes in which they were located. Most pastors were reluctant to have a convent close as that might mean the loss of sister-faculty, which created serious financial implications for them. To pay lay faculty was much more costly than to pay the sister-stipend.

I knew Father William Creed, the pastor of one of those parishes in question. Actually, I knew him from an earlier time as the moderator of the young adults' club to which I belonged prior to entering the convent. I had not seen him in many years and didn't really know him well, but I knew he was an open-minded and kind person with a compassionate love for the people with whom and for whom he served.

When I spoke with him, he shared my concern, but was also a bit reluctant to open the subject because he knew it would create uneasiness among the sisters and some parishioners as well. He had been assigned to the Black Parish where he was now located and was still reeling from the ravages of racial unrest that led to a massive exodus of White families from the parish as Black families began to immigrate. He was a man who loved peace, but he was also a man who loved the Gospel and had a strong orientation to justice. After our conversation, he agreed to host the meeting at his rectory. I invited the pastor of the other parish in question and the superiors of both convents for the discussion.

I arrived a bit early for the meeting and spoke briefly with Bill before the others arrived. Neither of us was very optimistic that anything would come of the discussion, except maybe to raise the level of awareness and concern. The conversation was pleasant but it was clear that no one wanted to take the discussion to the next level. No one wanted to offend the Sisters or jeopardize their well being. It was a situation I was experiencing too often — reluctance to change for fear of the repercussions. While I did not want to trample on people's feelings either, I was very impatient to make some changes that implemented the Gospel value of justice. I began to feel the status quo was becoming a straight jacket. I felt squeezed and crushed by its weight.

Weighing all the factors, I consulted with the other Provincial Team members. We agreed this was not the time to make the change in convent living; there were many other uncertainties. I called Bill Creed to communicate the decision. He was a wonderful listener and shared my frustration and disappointment. As we talked, I began to share with him my growing dissatisfaction with the pace of change in the Order. I did not want to leave, I assured him, but I felt I needed to make some adjustment in my life. I felt swallowed up in the narrowness and pettiness and dissension I found in my visits to the local houses. I desperately wanted to make a difference.

As we talked, I mentioned the possibility of being a candidate for the General Leadership Team, headquartered in Maryland. I had several opportunities to interact with members of the community from across the country. The General Chapter, to which I had been elected, brought together women from all nine provinces. They came from large and small cities, rural areas, farms, ranches, and migrant camps. They were from wealthy and poor families. This diversity made for lively and stimulating and sometimes frustrating conversations.

I expressed to him the joy and energy I felt when I was involved in those gatherings. I could feel myself coming alive even as I spoke with him. I chatted a bit more, closing the conversation by saying I needed to take some time to pray and discern what God wanted for me. He agreed but added, "I think you've already decided. I think you will leave yourself available for election, and I suspect you will be serving on the General Leadership Team after the Chapter."

I was breathless at his conclusion. I knew he was right. I was restless and needed to make a change if I was to continue to thrive in this life. It never occurred to me that I ought to reconsider my commitment to religious life. I was responding to God's will, and I would continue to do that, regardless of where it took me. I was elected to serve on the General Council. It meant I would move to the eastern city where the headquarters of the Order was located.

CHAPTER NINE

As I waited at the gate at O'Hare Airport, I was flooded with emotions that wrenched and saddened me. My family and a few of my friends came to see me off. The plane was delayed, an omen I hoped, and the waiting became interminable. This time the call of God was taking me far beyond anything I had known. I was leaving familiar terrain for totally new pathways. I was also caught up in the excitement of the journey that would open up broader perspectives and rich possibilities for growth.

When at last the signal was given to board, I said good-bye once again with tears and hugs and promises of prayers and letters and phone calls. As I approached the door to the boarding ramp, I felt panic and fear. What was I doing? Where was I going? How will it be so far away from family that I need to fly if there were an emergency? My legs wobbled briefly as I crossed the threshold. This was what God wanted for me and I would make it work. *It had worked until now hadn't it?*

When I reached my window seat, I looked back to the terminal to see if my family and friends were still visible. They were not and it was just as well. The door had barely shut when the pilot announced another delay due to needed repairs. *What does this mean? It certainly matches my reluctance to leave? Is this an omen? Will the plane make it? Is this where God is leading me now? Maybe I'm making too much of God's will.*

It was a very unsettled two hours before we took to the air for a flight that was pleasant and smooth, assisted by strong tail winds that made up some of the time lost at the gate. I expected Phyllis to meet me, but with this time change, there might be some confusion. I hoped someone would meet me as I was ready to get to my destination. It had been a long travel day already.

I was delighted to see Phyllis signaling me through the glass partition. I knew her best of the new team members, and I was already relaxed in her presence. She was bubbly, as usual, and very happy to see me.

"I'm so glad you're here. That building is like a mausoleum."

I wondered how it would be to live in that building when there were only a limited number of sisters in residence. Normally, when we were there more than one hundred women filled the halls and occupied the rooms on all three floors. Now, it would just be the five of us in a small wing on the second floor, and about fifteen others who occupied another wing of the building. Those sisters accepted responsibility for management of the building and grounds and a few taught in the school for special students on the same property.

I looked at Phyllis and said, "I was afraid of that. I'm so tired of living in institutions. I do like the fact that we're out in the country. It's lovely this time of year. And there is so much to see around the area."

In fact, she and I saw lots of the area searching out what might be of interest. There was really not enough for either of us to do when we arrived. Things had changed and the responsibility of the day-to-day decision making in the order had returned to the local provinces.

Structural changes attempted to respond to the new principles of subsidiarity and collegiality, outgrowths of Vatican II. Decisions formally relegated to the Mother General and her council were now handled at the local level, the level most affected by them. Permissions that previously needed approval from that level were no longer required. For example, it was no longer necessary for each convent to submit its daily schedule for approval. That kind of picayune administration wasted time and produced lots of paper.

The cessation of that activity left time for creative leadership, and I was looking forward to developing new roles. However, the other three members of the team who already had defined responsibilities did not sense the frustration that Phyllis and I experienced. I occupied an office but had very little to do. I made contacts with national organizations in the Washington area and hoped to find ways to connect with others who were taking peace and justice initiatives.

I felt inadequate and stagnant for the most part. I walked through the standing corn in the field adjacent to our building for long periods of time. *What am I doing here? Why was I called to this place? Is there a need for five people at this level any more? What is there to do? God, why am I here?* I walked a lot and questioned a good deal, but I had no answers. As trying as some of the responsibilities were in Chicago, I felt useful and productive. Here I felt useless and disconnected.

I felt frustration, disappointment and anger building in me. This was not a good sign, and I needed to do something to adjust the situation or myself. Through a mutual friend I made contact with a priest in the Washington area to pursue the questions I had in the context of spiritual direction.

When I arrived for my appointment with Father George O'Shea, I was bewildered somewhat. I had a brief exposure to spiritual direction. It was usually not something sisters engaged in as generally only priests or seminarians were considered suitable candidates for spiritual direction. That was beginning to change, though, and I sensed that George and I might have a longer-term relationship. If God was really involved in my life, I needed to get a handle on what and when and how to discern His plan for me.

Immediately, I felt a rapport with George. He encouraged me to call him by his first name as soon as we met. That helped to relax me. I blurted out in chaotic fashion all that was going on in my life. There had been so many changes in such a short time, and I was baffled by what it all meant. George was gentle and soft-spoken and listened with intense interest to my story. He seemed to understand some of the frustration I felt at being locked in place, so to speak. He, too, expressed some desire for more creative leadership in religious life. We agreed that I would undertake a more concentrated approach to prayer and meditation.

"God is calling you to something, Marsha, and you need to listen very carefully for the direction you are to follow."

There it was once again, the call of God. I felt some resentment toward George at that moment, but I couldn't just drop the idea. I intensified my efforts to pray and reflect and continued to meet with George once a month. Through the course of our meetings, I became clear about a direction for my life: spiritual leadership. *How do I do that? Where do I go for help?* An ad for a Masters Degree in Applied Spirituality caught my attention. The message resonated within my spirit, and I eagerly brought it to my next meeting with George. Without a moment's doubt, he encouraged me to apply and go from there.

The other team members supported me when I was accepted to participate in the four-summer program. It would mean some adjustments for them, of course, but they were willing to allow me to take this step. They had reservations, to be sure, but gave their blessing in the end.

The first summer was spent in a 30-day directed retreat. It offered an intense and powerful submersion into the life of Jesus and its intersection with my own. There was lots of silence, many hours of prayer and ample opportunity to swim and walk. I felt like a new woman when I returned to Maryland where the other sisters greeted me warmly and teased about how "holy" I looked. I confessed that was a bit of a stretch, but in fact, I had experienced some sort of significant change within.

I continued my meetings with George and began to hit my stride in terms of ministry and a role on the team. I was energized and enthusiastic once again. However, the impetus was not for a continued role in religious life leadership. I needed and wanted a broader experience of Church. When I completed my term in Maryland, I would seek ministry in parish, I thought. I was not prepared for the events that followed that spring.

CHAPTER TEN

I arrived at Chicago O'Hare on time, a rare occurrence at "The World's Busiest Airport." I was back in Chicago for the weekend to participate in the Chapter of Elections for the Province. I was very calm and peaceful as the plane traversed the miles, and I looked forward to seeing my family and friends. Opportunities to return home while I was in Maryland were rare, and when I did, the visits were short and too packed with people to see and places to visit. This weekend would be more of the same, I knew, but after only one more year in Maryland, I would come back to serve in some parish close to home, I thought.

I studied the list of nominees and thought about how I would vote, but I was eager to hear what was being said locally. It was difficult to stay on top of the current thinking being so far away. At least I could get some insights with Barbara and Janet who were meeting me at the plane. The procedure established by the election committee provided for nominations of candidates by all members of the province. Each nominee was then contacted to determine her willingness to be considered for election. I had been contacted and definitively declined.

I remembered that call several weeks earlier from Dorothy, a member of the election committee. I had already discussed the possibility with George and felt peaceful and resolute in my decision.

"Marsha, I'm calling because you have been nominated by a significant number of people in the province for the role of Provincial. I'm calling now to ask if you would leave your name in nomination."

"Dorothy, I've prayed about this and know it's not what I want to do. I have only one more year of my term here and plan to return to the province to do something entirely different. I've completed six years of community leadership responsibility and feel I need a change. I appreciate the vote of confidence from the sisters, but I am not willing to leave my name in nomination at this time."

I sensed her disappointment as she reluctantly acceded to my decision. Her voice sounded as though she had received a blow to the stomach.

"I'm terribly sorry you feel that way, Marsha. I guess I understand, but I'm not happy about it. Lots of others will be upset, too, as they are eager to have you return to Chicago. Many feel your talents are wasted out there."

"I just don't feel called to this role, Dorothy. I think Grace has done a fine job these past years, and I know she is eager to continue. What's the reason for dissatisfaction with her?"

"She's fine, but some people are ready for a change, someone with a new vision who is not so tied to the institutions we maintain."

I was relieved when our conversation ended and quietly savored the peace and freedom I felt. There was always some uncertainty in elections. Something unexpected could occur. While we believed the results were a reflection of the Will of the Spirit, political maneuvering was not uncommon. This was Chicago after all.

As I approached the baggage carrousel, I saw Barbara. She was waving frantically to get my attention. I was amazed to see how much weight she had lost. She looked great.

"Marsha, I have one bag with your name. Is that all you have?"

"Yes, I'm not staying long. You look great. How hard was it to get those pounds off?"

"It was excruciating! But tonight I'm not dieting. Janet and I want to take you to supper at the Italian Restaurant we always enjoyed."

"Where is Janet?"

"I imagine she is doing her best to avoid a parking ticket. She said she would pick us up right outside the door unless 'Chicago's finest' threatened to pounce like bloodhounds closing in on their prey."

Janet was right outside, and we were loaded and shortly on the way out of the Friday bustle typical of O'Hare. She swerved once to avoid the encroaching yellow cab, leaned on the horn and registered her displeasure. Once out of the area, we made good time and arrived at the restaurant with plenty of time for a relaxing dinner.

I was jolted by a comment Janet made as we approached the glass door of the restaurant.

"The election committee plans to submit a proposal to the eighty voting delegates tonight that would reopen the nomination process."

Some incredible uneasiness wound its way into my spirit. I felt panic and grabbed her by the arm. It seemed important to me to find out what she really was saying.

"I thought the nominations were closed. Why are they changing the rules now? That's not legitimate, is it?" My voice was strident. I was extremely agitated. *What was going on?* My stomach felt queasy, but I attributed that to the fact that I lunched on Eastern Time and was now in the Central Time Zone. *Maybe a little supper will calm my nerves. There is really nothing to worry about. You have made it clear to the election committee that you would not be available to serve in any position. No matter what they do to change the process, you don't have to change your decision.*

I don't know how much of my internal stirrings were apparent to them, but as soon as we took our seats at the table, I tried to make very clear that I was leaving community leadership when I finished at the Maryland office the next year.

"My decision is final, ladies. I've prayed about this and sorted all the dimensions through with George, my spiritual director, at length. I am really not available, and I would appreciate your spreading the word when we get to the Chapter. I've changed. I'm not the same person I was when I left the province two years ago," I said with conviction.

They looked at me intently and then turned to gaze at each other wondering, I thought, whether to pursue this change any further.

"Sure, Marsha, whatever you say. I'm not sure how many are really thinking about you as an add-on tonight. Relax. Let's eat, but sometime I'd like to talk with you about how you have changed," said Janet.

We moved on to various other topics as we downed our delicious meal. I felt myself becoming mellow. The robust red wine probably helped. We finished our meal and left the restaurant in plenty of time to make the drive to Ignatius High School, where the Chapter was being held. There were eighty delegates and close to one hundred observers in the room.

It resembled an active bee hive filled with the chatter of so many women. When we entered the room, several of my friends came over to greet me, happy that I was present for the elections and genuinely glad to see me. It was like a family reunion. Some of these women I knew well, others less. They were all good women, and I was happy to be connected to them.

The sound of the gavel on the podium preceded the call to order of Sister Miriam Louise, the chair of the election committee, who would preside over the events of this weekend.

"Will the delegates please come to order? We want to begin our deliberations as soon as possible."

Immediately, silence reigned and each of the delegates began to look for their places among the round tables that bad been distributed throughout the gym. My attention was drawn to a front table where Grace, the provincial, was signaling me. I was assigned to the same table with her. I thought she looked tired and perhaps tense, but she greeted me warmly.

She moved to the podium to call the Chapter to order and then invited the assembly to say the opening prayer:

"Come, Holy Spirit, fill the hearts of your faithful and kindle in them the fire of your love. Send forth your Spirit and they shall be created and You shall renew the face of the earth."

Miriam began, "Our first order of business is the proposal from the election committee which you have before you. As you know, it's important to keep the election process open to whatever the Spirit may be suggesting during the course of our deliberations. So, the committee felt it would facilitate matters if we could agree on a procedure to handle any new names that might surface tonight or tomorrow in the course of our voting.

"You each have a slate of names of sisters who have indicated they would serve if elected. However, we are not limited to those names only. In that way, we can comply with the norms of Canon Law regarding elections in religious communities."

"Must the person be present in the gym in order to be nominated?" Noreen O'Leary was always pretty careful about the details in any discussion.

"No. What the committee has suggested is that a person not presently on the ballot be contacted if she receives at least ten votes. If that would happen, a member of the election committee would contact the person to determine her preference. If the person is not in the room, we would make every reasonable attempt to reach her, but we will not delay the election if she is unable to be contacted. Is the proposal clear to everyone?"

Heads nodded in assent and an affirmative mumble could be heard in the gym.

"All those in favor of the proposal, please confirm."

The resounding response indicated the vote was favorable, but it was still necessary to ascertain if there were any in opposition. When that question was raised, the silence was clearly an indication that this proposal passed.

"The 'Ayes' have it," Miriam announced. "Let's proceed with the first ballot. As you know, this evening we will elect only the person who will serve as Provincial. The other six people will be elected tomorrow and Sunday."

Each wrote the name of the person we wanted to serve as provincial on slips of paper. Nothing had caused me to change my mind. As the ballots were collected and brought to the podium for counting, I caught Grace's eye and smiled supportively. She still looked very tense to me, but she returned my smile.

The atmosphere was electric, although there was absolute quiet in the room. No one was allowed to enter or leave the Chapter room during the counting of ballots. The formal process of recording the votes proceeded. With the ballots tallied, the Provincial came to the podium to read the names, beginning with the person receiving the least number of votes. There was a scattering of people with one or two nominations, another with three and a few more had four. Then I heard my name with eight votes. The remaining votes belonged to Grace, but they didn't constitute the two-thirds majority required for election. My heart was racing wildly. *This can't be happening. I'm not a nominee. I don't want to be a nominee. This is a terrible mistake.*

We moved to the second ballot, and the results required that the Chapter recess to determine the willingness of the person who received fifteen ballots —me.

"Sister Marsha Malone, will you allow your name to be considered for election?" Miriam asked.

I wanted to shout, "Absolutely not," but I felt I needed to take a few minutes to discern what this might be about. Was this now the Will of God for me?

"May I please have a few moments?" My body was agitated and once again I struggled with what I always believed: that my life was lived in response to the Call of God, a Call that was often not what I preferred. But I had been praying about this for a while. I talked with George at length. This just doesn't seem the right time for me.

The will of the community is the Will of God. I don't know that I still believed that from my early training. I heard the shuffling of feet and the strident rubbing of the gym chairs as they rubbed the gym floor. I had to offer some response soon. I reassured myself that I was a long way from the two-thirds majority and that I would not necessarily by elected if I did leave myself open. This just might be a message to Grace that people are not totally satisfied with her leadership.

I wanted desperately to leave the room, go to the bathroom or take a walk. *What's going on, God? What's happening? Please help me.*

I whispered hoarsely, my palms sweaty and my mind a jumble, "Yes, I will leave my name in nomination."

With that, Miriam announced the third ballot. When the votes were counted I received the necessary majority. I was in shock. My hands clenched tightly. I stared at Grace with disbelief as she moved to the podium to announce the results of the ballot.

"Sister Marsha Malone has been officially elected to serve as Provincial for the next three years."

As the gathered community broke into applause, Grace came to me and held me tightly. Her eyes welled with tears as she offered her congratulations. I felt awkward, uncomfortable and sad because I knew she was hurt. I hoped I had done the right thing and for a fleeting moment questioned how much of this was Spirit and how much the politics of election. In any case, the dye was cast, and the next three years would be very different than I had anticipated.

For the next hour or so, many well-wishers approached me and sounds of great joy came from others. Some were, of course, less than pleased, I knew. Grace's many friends in the Order, welcomed her style of leadership. Others, I sensed, were leery of me as they approached to offer the pro forma congratulatory greeting.

I was dazed, shocked, dismayed at what happened. Was this really what God wanted? On one hand, I was caught up in the excitement and enthusiasm; on the other I was fearful, even terrified of the consequences of this night. I felt suspended over an abyss.

CHAPTER ELEVEN

The remainder of the team of seven was elected the next day. That concluded the Chapter deliberations, freeing up Sunday for visiting with family and friends. I felt only minimally present to the conversations. I wanted to run from all that was happening. My parents were thrilled that I would be coming back to Chicago. I wanted to come back, but not like this. I was terrified of all that might be ahead in that role. I felt such conflict within. My prayer became simply one of surrender to God's will. My heart, however, continued to wonder how much was God's will and how much was the politics of elections. I couldn't wait to board the plane and return to Maryland.

I was still shaken when I arrived at Dulles Airport on Sunday evening. The other four members of that team greeted me at the gate. Bewildered, they wanted to know the details. All they knew was that I had been elected. Consuela, the Superior General, spoke first. She was usually calm and gracious, but she seemed agitated now. "Marsha, how are you? What happened out there? We were dumbfounded when the call came Friday night. When do you have to leave here? What will we do about replacing you?"

Always an eager and efficient administrator, she began planning the next steps on Friday night. I, on the other hand, had no idea about anything that would come next.

"I honestly haven't even thought about it. When I left here, I was a free spirit with no intention of becoming involved in the election. You know, I really want to do Spiritual Direction and Retreat Work in a parish when I finish here. That's why I've been doing the summer program at the University. I feel overwhelmed by all this."

Our conversation continued throughout the ride home and during the festive dinner they planned to celebrate my election. Consuela was a marvelous hostess and loved fancy dinners. We had many of them throughout my two years. This one was not without its down side—my leaving and the necessity of finding another person to complete my term. That would affect the dynamics of the Team and would offer a challenge and opportunity they would have preferred to avoid. My concerns continued to flow during the course of dinner.

"I have so little energy for internal community business. You are aware of some of the ways in which I've changed. I know I've caused you a good deal of frustration with my impatience with the slow pace I felt we took regarding implementing justice. I'm not looking forward to trying to create change at the Province either. It's always such a struggle to do that."

Donna thought it might be possible to modify the role that the Provincial generally assumed, make it more spiritual leadership and less administrative.

"You're so good at bridging and healing, Marsha," volunteered Jenna. "I'm sure you'll do fine."

The next morning, at our regular weekly meeting, we began to plan for the next steps. My heart was not in the replacement process. I knew whoever was selected would carry on in fine style. My preoccupation now was trying to get a handle on some of the details and difficulties I would face as I assumed my new role. It became necessary to travel to Chicago several times during those three months so that the transition between groups could be handled as smoothly as possible.

Grace recovered her stride and greeted me graciously each time I arrived for the meeting. She was kind and supportive in her orientation to the role. I was very uncomfortable with the situation and told her.

"I'm so sorry this happened, Grace. You know I did not want this role. I don't even know whether I can do it well. I am quite satisfied with your leadership."

"It's not your decision, Marsha. The province apparently is not satisfied with what I am doing, and I can't really function in that environment. You'll be fine and I'll gladly help, but I would prefer you not draw me into Province affairs, unless it is absolutely necessary."

Her pain was almost tangible and I ached for her, but I knew it would take some time for her to heal from the hurt and humiliation she experienced. Fortunately, she had been accepted for a sabbatical program in another state, and she looked forward to beginning. That would give her some distance and also make the transition easier for me.

So much enthusiasm was evident in the province when the new team began to function. Momentarily, it rekindled the energy and passion for religious community leadership I thought I had lost. *Maybe God is really in this process after all.* I readily established my style and presence and felt receptivity to my shift in focus from serving on Boards of Directors and Administration to Spirituality and Community. The changes that occurred as a result of Vatican II and our own subsequent Community Chapters created further divisions among the sisters in the Province.

"There are lots of hurting people out there, Marsha. And we need to give them our priority," Brigid said.

She was one of the team members I was least comfortable with but I didn't know why. I fought my suspicions in order to remain open to her insights and experience. Her lack of support for my continuing to pursue the program in spiritual leadership that summer added fuel to the smoldering unrest I felt. I had communicated my strong desire to continue the spirituality program to the province at the time of the election, and there seemed to be no resistance to being away for the six weeks. Now, as I planned to cover my responsibilities in anticipation of leaving, I heard reluctance from the team.

"The Sisters won't understand why you're away for six weeks just after beginning your term. They will be very upset. We need you here this year. Put off your program for another year," urged Brigid.

"Well, if we are going to work as a team, then we might just as well start now. Each of you has an area of responsibility, and I would like to encourage the province members to approach you with their concerns about ministry, finances, community living, or education. Many are away from the Province for study and/or vacation. You know how slow things are over the summer. In light of the unanticipated change due to the election, I really feel I need to take the time this summer to focus on the spiritual dimensions of our life."

I felt a bit shaky and silently wondered if that was the right move. When the others responded affirmatively, I stayed the course and return to the program in California.

The woman who assumed the role of Assistant Provincial was a very good friend and a very capable person to assume some of my responsibilities for the summer. She was involved in a creative project, a holdover from the previous administration, and felt quite confident she could pursue it until my return. She definitely felt I needed to become involved upon my return, as the implications were far-ranging.

Actually, the project seemed fairly benign in terms of potential conflict, I thought. There was in Chicago an urgent need for housing for seniors. We had been approached by a representative of Catholic Charities and another from the Jewish Council for the Elderly and listened carefully and enthusiastically to their proposal. We agreed to sell one of the half-empty dormitory buildings on the campus of our college. Carmen was designated as our contact with the group. I looked forward to the time when I could be involved as well.

I was totally taken back when I received a frantic phone call from Carmen, shortly after I began the summer program. The positive dimensions we anticipated crashed into a solid wall of opposition. The local pastors of the Catholic Churches in the area were contacted by the priest-director of Catholic Charities so that he might explain the plans. They became irate. They should have been contacted before any approach was made to the Sisters. There is a line of command in the Catholic Church that is hierarchical and clerical and this violated the protocol.

As word began to filter to the people through the local papers who heralded this as a disaster being foisted on the southwest side by the Sisters, there was a huge outcry.

Carmen was almost frantic when she called me that night. She was stunned and horrified by what was being said and done to prevent the continuation of this project.

"Marsha, I wish you were coming soon. This has gotten out of hand. We're dealing with racism and its full fury. No one has used that label, but that is what it is. I can't believe this, truly. Some of our sisters are involved, too, enraged that we caused such a disruption in the lives of family members who live in the area. Today, the representatives for the proposal and I met with the local cluster of pastors. It was just awful. The only one who was supportive was Bill Creed."

I had never heard Carmen so overwrought, and I knew this must have been a horrendous encounter. I was not surprised at the support of Bill Creed. I knew him, of course, and recognized him as a pastor open to new ideas and one who rejected pomp and protocol. He was often a lone voice at those pastoral gatherings.

"Do you think this is a dead issue, Carmen?"

"I certainly hope not but I think we need to delay further discussion until you return. I'm not too sure where the other team members are on this right now. They don't like the uproar."

"Well, take care. We'll get on this together, my friend."

At the first team meeting after my return, we talked at length about the positive aspects we envisioned when we initially considered this proposal. It would provide safe housing for seniors, offer opportunities for their continuing education at the college, and create some jobs for students and ministry for the many retired sisters who lived on that same campus.

Our strategy began with an approach to Bill Creed to get us on the agenda for the next meeting of pastors. He was only able to get us fifteen minutes at their meeting two weeks hence. Gracious at first, the pastors' tone gradually became more tense and angry. The sisters should never even have considered this proposal until the pastors made a decision about it.

"Sisters, if you asked us first we could have saved you a lot of grief," the chairman began very condescendingly. "We know our people and understand their sufferings and fear about this proposed change."

Another added with smugness and superiority, "There is a line of authority in the Church and you would have done well to have observed it."

I felt diminished and dismissed and that made me very angry, but I didn't feel this was the time to address my concerns about hierarchy and clericalism. I held fast to the arms of the chair to restrain my emotions. Then I heard Bill Creed begin to speak, very convincingly, I thought. His was the lone voice of support, and I admired his courage in countering his fellow clerics.

Our time was over and we were dismissed from the room. Bill escorted us to the door and asked us to meet him shortly for lunch at a near-by restaurant. He felt the meeting would finish soon, and he really wanted to talk more with us about what had happened.

We were both elated to have an opportunity to talk with someone who might have some insight into what all the fuss was about. Neither of us was very sympathetic to the clergy who felt the institution was theirs alone.

Carmen and I sipped large iced teas and vented our feelings. Within a very short time, Bill arrived, looking chagrined at the turn of events.

"Bill thanks so much for your support. We really appreciate your help," Carmen said with feeling. She and Bill had been friends for quite a few years, since they were assigned to the same parish when Bill was newly ordained and Carmen was on her first assignment.

"The pastors were gracious, Bill, but they are so stuck in their clerical roles," I said. "Is it such a big deal that they weren't approached first? What a power play. I hoped if we talked with them and shared the proposal, they might lessen their resistance. Today's session convinces me that I was terribly wrong," I said with resignation.

"I'm sorry nothing changed. I've been trying to talk this up informally, but you know they all refer to me as 'Black Bill'."

Carmen and I howled. "Black Bill" was a ruddy-complexioned red head who happened to be pastor of the only Black parish in that cluster. He told us he was accustomed to feeling disregarded when he attended meetings, but he continued to go because he felt it was important to speak for the population of Black parishioners he served. It seemed women were not the only ones disregarded by the church.

CHAPTER TWELVE

When we returned to the Provincial House, we shared with the other team members our conclusion that we would not receive any support from the local pastors for this project. We hoped this might be a moment of grace for the pastors who could use this as an opportunity to deal with the racial tensions that ran rampant in the southwest side of the city. The migration of Blacks generated anger and animosity with many of their parishioners and the area was a volatile one, ripe for violent reactions whenever people gathered. Someone needed to intervene and try to break new ground, but that was not going to be done by the pastors at this time.

My next hope was to try to persuade Cardinal Carey of the importance of this housing project. Perhaps he would use his persuasive power with the clergy to turn the tide. I sent him a letter in which I explained what we hoped to do and asked for a meeting to discuss ministerial implications of this project. After all, I reminded him in the letter, he was the person who was primarily responsible for the development of ministry in the

Archdiocese. Upon receipt of my letter, he called to schedule an appointment.

Carmen and I journeyed together to the Chancery Office in downtown Chicago. When we arrived at the large, modern, brick building, we opened the heavy glass door and moved across the empty lobby to the receptionist who directed us to the fifth floor. Neither of us had been to this newly-built Chancery Building, and we were quite impressed by its size and the marble appointments. We exited the elevator and confronted another set of doors where a woman sorted some files. She greeted us and escorted us to the wooden door that opened to a very large office.

The Cardinal was standing behind his very imposing mahogany desk and greeted us graciously as we did him. Carmen and I were totally surprised to see a number of rather grim-looking men on both sides of him. The desk was large enough so each of them could share a piece of the wooden desk-top. In front of each of them was a large stack of papers. As Cardinal Carey introduced each one, he gave us their official title and outlined their responsibility. He turned to us, then, and I began. "Cardinal Carey, we appreciate your prompt response to our request about this housing for the elderly project. We anticipate new ministries that could develop for many of our sisters who reside on that campus." I wasn't sure just how much he knew about the difficulties that existed between the clergy and the province in regard to this project, so I chose to avoid the topic unless he addressed it.

"I'm sure there will be new developments, Sister, but there are necessary forms you needed to complete and forward to this office for approval of the sale of that property. If we concur with your decision, we will send the forms to Rome. I have asked Mr. Genera and Mr. Handily to gather the documents for you," the Cardinal Archbishop said. With that, he turned to the man immediately to his right.

"Will you please explain the necessary steps to the Sisters?"

Carmen and I looked at each other with amazement. Our letter of request had said nothing about finances. We were there to talk with him about ministry.

"Oh, but Cardinal, the property has already been sold. Our Board of Advisors and the Chapter Delegates approved the sale several months ago," I added quickly. I became apprehensive that this might become difficult, and I wasn't ready for another confrontation about this project.

"Our advisors have wonderful expertise in the matter of finances and they were very enthusiastic about this proposal," Carmen added.

In fact, they had scrutinized the proposal and examined the contract for any possible financial loopholes on the part of either Catholic Charities or the Jewish Council for the Elderly. Their concern was not for the ministry, as such, but for the fiscal security of the Province.

The Cardinal became visibly upset, pounded his desktop once and then gathered the papers in front of him into his arm. His voice was strident and his chair flew away from him as he stood from the desk.

"What? How could you do that? You did not receive permission from this office. No wonder Rome is so concerned about religious women in this country."

We chose to let that last comment pass, already too aware of the restrictiveness with which the Institution attempted to deal with religious communities of women. We were addressing some of our concerns and responses in our national meetings.

I was hesitant and a bit fearful of repercussions as I responded to the accusation of failed paper work.

"It really doesn't make sense to write Rome about a property sale in Chicago. They aren't in a position to know whether or not it is viable. We came because we wanted to talk with you about this ministry that we know is of such vital importance to you," I said, tongue in cheek. In truth, his primary concern since he came to Chicago had been financial solvency.

We knew we would break new ground in finalizing the transaction without Vatican approval. There was a decided difference of opinion in the Church over whether the sale of property that belonged to a religious community was subject to Canon Law and, therefore, required Vatican approval. We knew we were bound by American Civil Law. We consulted with experts in both fields and concurred with their conclusion that Canon Law was not relevant in our situation. The difference of opinion continued to this day, more than twenty years later.

His back to us, the Cardinal began his exit and turned his head to Mr. Handily advising him to give us the necessary paper work. He bellowed at us over his shoulder.

"When you fill out these forms, I'll do what I can to try to rectify this with Rome. Then we'll talk about ministry."

His henchmen followed him from the room, and Carmen and I were soon alone in the spacious, well-appointed office. We took our first in-depth look and were stunned to see the lavish décor of this new headquarters. There was nothing there to interest us, so we left quietly, taking the envelope, knowing we would not comply with his request.

We did not try to be deliberately difficult, but there were principles involved here, and we felt we needed to do what we could to implement them. When the Vatican Council introduced principles of subsidiarity, they intended that decision making in the Church would be made at the level most affected by the decision. That principle struggled to breathe new life into the institutional operation. It also threatened the rigid hierarchical structure that was in place.

CHAPTER THIRTEEN

Convinced it was necessary and viable, we decided to try one more time to save this project for elderly housing. We contacted our local alderman, who sat on some of our Boards, and asked him to schedule us on a City Council agenda. I knew from stories in the press that he did not favor this project, but his loyalties to the Order gave him the impetus to follow through on this request.

The day Carmen and I arrived at City Hall, we were confronted by a large, boisterous group of people who learned of our scheduled appearance before the Aldermen.

"There they are. Why are you doing this? You know we don't want it."

"Go home and take care of your own business."

Boos and jeers echoed in the marbled stairwell.

I was very uneasy, and even a bit frightened at the intensity of this opposition. The setting itself was intimidating and formal but the shouting and jeering of the mostly female crowd was overwhelming. The Council clerk came to the lobby and escorted us into the Chambers. Perhaps now we would find calm and peace as we sought to explain what we were trying to do.

I took some deep breaths in the momentary calm, soon interrupted by the shuffling of feet and chairs in the balcony. I turned from the holding booth where we sat and recoiled from the sight of the angry, hate-filled faces.

I whispered to Carmen, "God, I don't know if I can get through this. Look at that crowd."

"You'll be fine. Don't look up there. Try to find one friendly face and focus on it."

The Chairman announced our topic and invited me to come forward to speak. The balcony rocked with shouts as the parliamentarian and sergeant-at-arms tried in vain to quiet the crowd. They were finally able to quiet them when the chairman threatened to expel them from the room. They had made their point, though, and I had no doubt they affected the Council members.

The outcome of the discussion with the Council was to refer it to the Zoning Board. They were instructed to schedule an open hearing in the local community at a date and time convenient to them. The chairman thanked us for coming and said to expect a notice of when and where the meeting would take place.

In the intervening weeks, the fires of racism stirred the people in that southwest side area to action. They organized and rallied the troops by generating fear that this all-white neighborhood would be overtaken by Blacks. This fear was fueled by the fact that this project, like all similar projects during that era, would require Housing and Urban Development approval, which would necessitate the inclusion of a diverse racial population. They did not hear that the residents would all be elderly, only a very small percentage minorities. Black bashing was the rage at that time. Unwittingly I had entered into a hornet's nest.

At the appointed date and time, I arrived at the meeting site and was floored when I saw the enormity of the crowd that turned out for the hearing. My heart raced wildly as I attempted to slip in the open door past large men who guarded the entrance to the already over-crowded room. I knew no one, as far as I could see, and apparently no one recognized me as yet. I was terrorized by the comments that scorched the air.

"They'll come in here to visit their parents and grandparents and rape our daughters on the way out."

"The Sisters have betrayed us. We supported them all through the years and now this is what they're doing to us. That's the last they'll see of our money."

"I talked with our pastor and he told me there will be no such development taking place. Apparently, they never even bothered to go through proper channels."

"We'll need additional sewers. Who's going to pay for that?"

The voices in the room reached fever pitch, and I became more and more frightened. No other members of the province team were free to attend this meeting. There was a large concentration of our sisters in that area, but none of them came. I searched frantically for a familiar or friendly face, and there in the back of the room was the smiling countenance of one of our older sisters. I wished I could have run to her to thank her for being there. I knew I would never forget her for coming. She was the only friendly face in the entire room.

Finally, the Zoning Committee member who would chair the meeting arrived. The atmosphere became even more volatile and intense. People shouted across the room to their neighbors. The volume was ear-shattering. I looked to Sister Laverne and saw her face tightening. She was scared to death, I knew, and so was I.

The chairman finally arranged everything and began the meeting trying to say the purpose for the gathering, but hardly anyone was listening. He called me to the speaker's stand and my knees buckled as the room exploded with boos, jeers and condemnations, the like of which I had never experienced. It took many minutes before the group was calmed and quieted.

"I'm here because I want to try to dispel the rumors and ..." The mob broke in. "Turn the property into a cemetery." "We don't want that monstrosity in our neighborhood." "You have betrayed us."

Once again the room rocked. I was really terrified as I looked at some of the faces of the almost two hundred men and women jammed into the small classroom. Some sat, most stood and shouted, crowded against one another to accommodate to the limited space. I desperately wanted to run for the nearest exit and saw that I was literally trapped, held captive by this crowd. I have never been so afraid, fearing even for my life. This was no longer a gathering of concerned people. It was a mob. The situation was volatile—anything could happen.

I was dazed, exhausted and totally overwhelmed. I don't remember how the meeting ended or how I was able to escape. I got into my car, sobbing and shaking. I had to get going away from here, but I didn't feel safe to drive. I have never been so frightened. The fear that someone might come after me prompted me to turn the ignition and head for home.

As promised, I called Bill. He answered on the first ring. I knew he was expecting my call. We had talked about his coming to the meeting but felt it would be counter-productive and might even be dangerous for him. Some of those in the crowd would recognize him. It wasn't that he was afraid. He had experienced many difficult meetings with present and former parishioners, and he knew the fury of racism first hand.

I knew my voice was shaky, and I struggled to hold back the tears that rushed to my eyes when I heard his voice. I explained as best as I could what happened and began to sob.

"Marsha, I am so sorry I was not there with you. I wish I had gone. I'm so sorry. Would you like me to come by, maybe have a bite of supper? Is there anything I can do for you?" He was urgent and insistent but wanted to respect my wishes for time alone.

I was exhausted and wanted nothing more than to rest and regroup, although I didn't know if I could. I thanked him profusely as I refused his offer. I promised to call him in a couple of days. Part of me didn't want him to hang up. His voice was such a comfort. *Where was that coming from? Was I so desperate for a kind word after the horror of the afternoon or was he becoming someone important and special to me?*

CHAPTER FOURTEEN

During the weeks following this fiasco at the Zoning Board hearing, I waited for final word, but I knew the outcome was written on the wall already. Carmen and I had spent quite a bit of time and energy on this and were not at all hopeful, but very disappointed. *How could something that seemed destined to bring so much good be arousing such negative responses?*

I talked with Bill one day about my frustration and then recalled how I became so aware of racial bigotry earlier in my life. Growing up in Chicago in the '50s thrust me into a hot bed of racial tensions. This major metropolitan city was one of the most racially segregated areas in the country. Ethnic barriers existed, to be sure, but the geographical separation of Blacks and Whites in terms of housing was normative. Blacks generally congregated on the near West and South sides of the city. While those boundaries remained rigid, there were no overt problems.

However, as more Blacks migrated from the South in pursuit of jobs, homes and security, the boundaries became fluid and penetrable, but not without great difficulty. The powerful mayor of the city, Richard X. Delany, was steadfast in his commitment to preserve the status quo in terms of segregation. The local papers carried articles almost daily of Black families' frustrated attempts to find homes in the White communities. Cursing, fire and violence erupted wherever there was an attempt to move into the White neighborhoods. These experiences brought to light latent and repressed tensions.

Groups tried to form compassionate outreach to those disenfranchised by their Race. People of mixed racial groups gathered where members might get to know one another as persons. Friendship House was an organization operative in the city, and it sought to form many such gatherings. I participated in many sessions, and it opened me to the futility of that type of group affecting appropriate changes.

I internalized the conviction that structures needed to change in order to enhance people's quality of life. I was appalled as I sat in the Catholic Church we attended when the pastor promised our congregation that no Blacks would invade our parish as long as he was in charge. That was his attempt to assuage the grief and fear of our all-White congregation as our borders became porous.

In truth, the Black people did not invade our parish. The Catholic Church in our city at that time was determined to maintain its segregated stance. As a result, few Blacks became or remained Catholic. However, the migration continued in spite of their opposition. The houses on our block soon became home to some Black families. My family welcomed our neighbors and found them an asset to our small community. We were content to share life with persons whose skin color was darker than ours but who shared a similar goal for maintaining the neighborhood.

Our lack of financial resources, no doubt, kept us open and accepting to the changes we faced. We could not afford to move. That determination to remain was weakened when the boy next door, a Black young man of my age, asked me to go to a movie.

My parents were adamant in their resistance. They liked Joe; we all did. He was an asset to our baseball team and a very polite young man. Their fear, although I was only twelve, was expressed to neighbors who gathered on our front porch in the evening. I overheard my dad one night as I passed the screen door to go upstairs to bed, "Would you want your daughter to marry a Black?"

I told Joe I was unable to go to the movie because my parents didn't want me to date yet. We both knew the real reason but were in no position to challenge it. We continued to play ball together, but there was a new undercurrent in the group. The White boys, told by my brother of the invitation by Joe, came to resent his boldness in approaching one of their own. Very soon, I learned that we were preparing to move farther West in the city.

That move temporarily gave us a "conflict-free" racial environment, but it did not dispel my concern about the injustice and inequality in our city and church. In the next several years I began a letter-writing campaign to the editors of our daily and archdiocesan newspapers. A few of them were published. That was the extent of my work for justice at that time in my life.

Entrance into the Order and subsequent years of formation did not allow for any involvement with activity that was erupting across the city and the country. The Civil Rights Movement, inspired by Dr. Martin Luther King and the March on Selma began to impact our religious congregation. A number of professed sisters agitated with authority for the opportunity to participate in the Selma March. I would have loved to join, but was prohibited because of my status as a temporary professed sister. I followed the events very closely, and they stirred my soul.

One of my hopes as I grew to maturity and became involved in leadership in the Order was to influence structural change. That was clearly my dream as I assumed the responsibility of the role of provincial. This first test case, the housing for the elderly project, whetted my appetite even further. However, the project failed.

The local pastors had their say with the Cardinal, presumably sharing their complaints at having been bypassed in the initial consideration. Many of the people present at the hearings further persuaded them that the development of this project would cost the parishes in the long run as they would no longer support them financially.

Many of our own sisters were upset as they listened to the outpourings of persons in their schools opposed to the project. They voiced their opposition to the Provincial Team. The final blow was the recommendation from the Zoning Board to the City Council that this initiative should be defeated; and it was.

For a while, routine province business occupied a great deal of my time. In some ways, it was a relief to have a cessation to all the turmoil. The maintenance of province-sponsored institutions, financial concerns about caring for a growing elderly membership, provision of health care for our sisters now that third-party payers were involved in our hospitals, and most importantly, attention to the spiritual, physical and emotional well being of the sisters in the province occupied most of my time.

While province business became routine, my personal life became challenging. Bill and I found each other kindred spirits as a result of our meetings and interactions. We found comfort and strength in each other as we worked with groups in the Archdiocese on issues important to us. It was an invigorating experience for both of us, and we relished our friendship, oblivious to the potential consequences.

CHAPTER FIFTEEN

The relationship started so innocently. Bill would celebrate Mass for our community on different occasions. I greatly admired the style and delivery of his homilies at Mass and his non-clerical style of presiding at liturgies. He came across as warm and sensitive, and he clearly took time to prepare, which was not always a given with clergy-celebrants of liturgy. I appreciated that very much.

I also valued his convictions about issues facing the Church. He believed as I did, there was a pressing need for thinking more creatively about racism, housing for the elderly and women in the church. I looked forward to the meetings on these topics, hoping Bill would be there. After a while, we began to wait for each other after a meeting just to chat. I enjoyed conversations with him. I suspected we shared a great deal in common and wondered if we would ever become friends. I would not take the initiative to pursue this; he had a great reputation as a good priest, and I didn't know how he felt about friendships with women.

After one of the meetings we both attended, Bill asked,

"Marsha, are you free to have lunch one day this week? There's something I'd like to talk with you about."

I was flattered, excited and curious. *What could be on his mind?* "Sure, Bill, I have time for lunch. Either Wednesday or Friday would be best for me. Is either of those good for you?"

When he arrived at the Provincial House on the designated day, he was dressed in his full clerical suit. It was pretty common for priests at that time to wear "civvies" when they were doing social activities, so they would not draw attention to themselves. When we arrived at the restaurant, Bill spotted two priests he knew and went to speak with them. When he returned, he commented, "I'm glad I wore my clerics. They won't think something is going on between us."

Since there was nothing going on, except the possibility of becoming friends, I was a bit puzzled by his comment. It was common knowledge that priests were developing close personal relationships with women and that some moved beyond the boundaries of celibacy. I even counseled a few members of religious communities who were engaged in that type of relationship. This was not what was happening with us. We were only acquaintances with a great deal in common.

As we proceeded to enjoy our lunch, Bill volunteered the reason for his invitation. He explained that he was having a difficult time relating to a member of the faculty of his school. Since she was someone I knew, he thought I might have some insight to offer that would assist him in bridging the conflict. We covered a variety of topics and discovered how much we agreed regarding our dreams and vision for religious life, priesthood and Church.

When we returned to the Provincial House, Bill suggested we might do the lunch thing again and we did, rather soon. Before we knew it, we were having lunches, occasional dinners, walks in the woods and along the shores of Lake Michigan, and even a play or two. We both loved tennis and played regularly, sometimes just the two of us, other times, with a priest and nun who were good friends and a married couple Bill knew.

We contacted each other when either of us was involved in preparing talks, homilies, retreats, or other public presentations. Bill was the kind of priest who was always looking for ways to open his parishioners to their own gifts and goodness. He would often test his ideas with me before exploring their possibility with the parish. He was active in Cursillo, a personal renewal experience that was becoming popular in the Archdiocese. Bill was often invited to be the presiding chaplain on those weekends. We spent many hours developing ideas for his presentations.

Whenever I needed to deliver a major talk for my community or facilitate a retreat, I made certain that we had time to explore the implications of what I would say. We found such comfort and support in those opportunities shared. Each of us felt somewhat alone in our hopes and desires, and it was wonderful to explore new ground with such a thoughtful and caring person.

I don't know when I became aware that I loved him, but I knew my feelings for him were deeper and stronger than before. I felt Bill was feeling somewhat the same, but we didn't really talk about it until one day as we riding in his car and a favorite song of both of us came on the radio, "There's a time for us, somewhere a time for us..."

Bill turned from the road to look at me. "You know, Marsha, lately I find myself singing along with the music of some of the songs on the radio, so many of them remind me of you and the time we have together. I don't know how to explain it. I just know there's something much more alive in me. I look forward to seeing you, talking with you, being with you, even thinking about you. I know something very good has happened for me, and I hope that's true for you."

I was shaken, my heart racing and my palms sweaty. "I think I know what you mean, Bill. I'll be involved in something and all of a sudden my attention will shift to thoughts of you and something you said, something we shared. I feel much more peaceful and happy than I ever have."

It was out there now, and it felt good to finally be able to talk with him about what I was feeling — the emotional highs, the energy, the loneliness when we were apart. "I hesitated to tell you, Bill, because I was afraid you might not want to continue to spend time with me. I know you love being a priest, and I'm happy in my life. I've never felt this way before. I really want to continue to deepen our friendship, and I think we can do that and still remain true to who we are."

Bill agreed and confirmed how much his life as priest and his ministry meant to him. "I was becoming depressed, though, until I started to spend time with you. I felt pretty alone until I met you. Your friendship means so much to me. I've always had great respect for you, and I support what you are trying to do in your community. I know it's a hard road."

I was elated to realize we were becoming good friends. I knew we would need to be cautious and guarded in our expressions of affection. We had seen people go down the road and over the edge. We did not want that to happen. Holding hands on our walks and hugging whenever we parted was the extent of our expression of affection. I was happy and content and found some of my tasks less burdensome.

Gradually, our expressions became more romantic. I remember the wonder and awe of our first kiss. It occurred in winter, a particularly snowy one. Bill suggested we take a whole day away together to do some cross-country skiing. I had never done that and it sounded like fun. He arranged for a room at a resort where we could change clothes and relax before and after skiing. I felt a twinge of apprehension when he told me about the room, but he assured me it would be more convenient. I trusted him, but maybe wasn't too sure about myself. I couldn't imagine we would do anything inappropriate physically. I had so many restrictions around sexuality in my psyche, having been educated in Catholic schools all my life. Plus, I was a nun and fully intended to remain faithful to my commitment. We politely and carefully allowed each other the opportunity to change clothes and headed for the pro shop to get fitted with shoes and skis.

The outdoor air was crisp and clear. The resort was virtually empty and the ski trails well groomed. We wound through woods, along a stream, up and down some gently-sloped hills, and some not-so-gentle ones. I fell a few times but Bill was always there to assist me to my feet. He was such a strong and gentle man.

The day was marvelous. After we skied a while, we stopped for lunch, and then returned to the ski trails again. In the late afternoon, we returned to the room where we showered and changed. We stretched out on the two beds in the room and talked for a couple of hours. I could hardly believe what a wonderful gift of friendship I had received. Bill was so interested in what I cared about. He enjoyed listening to my plans and dreams. He had shared with me months earlier how much he valued my listening to him. There was a new intimacy developing that day, but I just wanted to enjoy the moment. So far, everything was going just fine.

As we drove home that evening, I was euphoric. Words flowed easily. There was no awkwardness or anxiety, only the hope that we could prolong the feeling as long as possible. We were basically shy and reserved socially. We chatted away with buoyancy and delight. It was so wonderful to be known and heard and respected by another. I hated to see the day end and hoped Bill felt the same. A short distance from my home, Bill pulled over to the curb in front of a paint store on one of the main streets.

"Today was wonderful, Marsha. I love our times together." He paused, hesitant to go on, but then he said, "Sometimes I think I want more."

Panic invaded my bones and I cautiously asked what he meant, hoping this would not change the wonderful friendship we were developing. I was not prepared to respond to any request that would take me beyond the commitment I had. I wasn't looking for anything like that and quickly reassured myself that Bill was strong and faithful to his commitment, too.

I turned to look directly into his eyes, hoping my uneasiness was not too obvious.

"What do you mean, Bill?"

"Well, like tonight, I really would like to kiss you. I wanted to do that all day, especially in the room, but I didn't want to do anything to make you uncomfortable."

I recalled wanting to hold or hug him, too. It was probably just as well. It was safer here in the car.

With premature relief, I responded, "I'd like to kiss you, too, very much."

We moved closer and kissed each other gently and warmly for the first time. My heart exploded with sound and color. This moment of intimacy touched the depths of my spirit. Our heavy winter jackets proved cumbersome, but they didn't diminish the closeness we felt as we continued to hold each other in awe and amazement. My heart pounded with delight, and I couldn't imagine ever feeling happier than I did at that moment.

Bill spoke quietly. "Is that your heart or mine that is beating so loudly?"

"I think it's both our hearts," I whispered.

We continued to hold each other a while longer, feeling the warmth of our love. I knew we had moved beyond anything I anticipated or imagined. The emotions awakened in me were so powerful that I couldn't think life would ever be the same again. I wondered where this evening would take us. It was enough just to be so happy and so loved. I wondered how Bill was feeling now.

"Marsha, ever since you came into my life, I've known we were heading into a very deep and loving relationship. In my quiet times after we have been together, I would hear myself saying to you, 'Get out of my life, but don't you dare.' I'd be crushed if something was to happen, and we would no longer be friends."

"I know you're the most important person in my life right now. I miss you terribly when we are apart for any length of time. I, too, would be lost without you, but we have to make this fit into the rest of our life. I think we can do it, don't you?"

"I sure want to, Marsha."

That seemed to break the spell, and we moved away from each other as if to state with our bodies our resolution to keep this together.

We pulled up to my door in a few minutes. As I prepared to leave the car Bill said, "I'm so glad I had the courage to ask you for that kiss. It was just wonderful, like I imagined it would be — warm and cozy. Thanks, Marsha, for a great day. When can we get together again?"

We set a time and I kissed him briefly on the cheek and moved to my door. I was lifted along by the power of our joining. I hoped I would not betray all that I was feeling to those with whom I lived. They would, no doubt be waiting for my return, interested in how the day went, and possibly concerned by the development of this friendship. I gave them a brief account of the day and excused myself since I was tired and anticipated a full schedule the following day. In reality, I wanted to be alone to savor and reflect on what had happened.

On the way to work the next morning, I took a route that would allow me to revisit the scene of the previous night. I looked across at the storefront window and was amazed to see that its glass pane was cracked diagonally. I chuckled at the power of that kiss. I had no idea what caused the crack, but it seemed to me it might have been the impact of our kiss.

When I got to the office I called Bill to tell him about the glass, but he had already seen it—he revisited the scene earlier. We laughed and laughed, oblivious to the implications of the intensification of our relationship. It would shatter forever the window from which each of us viewed our world, one that was devoid of this kind of passion. Our celibate life style had not prepared us for the awesomeness of our love; in fact, it labeled such love illicit. We did not know at that moment how we would integrate this, but we knew it was very important to continue to explore the meaning of each other in our lives. The crack in the window exposed the fragile nature of our existence.

CHAPTER SIXTEEN

I was disenchanted with how much time and energy was spent on maintenance of institutions and sponsored ministry, facilitating internal divisions and tensions, recruitment and training of new members (a smaller number requiring a greater investment of personnel, I thought), planning for the increasing population of our community that was reaching retirement age and over-all operation of the province.

While I was frightened and anxious about the directions we pursued toward racial equality, I found much more energy and enthusiasm in those endeavors. Many changes loomed ahead for the church and the city of Chicago, and I felt it was important to be involved where we could. So I continued to bring critical issues to our team for some sort of action.

Following the failure of the housing for the elderly proposal and the obvious racist bigotry that created the situation, Carmen and I felt we must initiate some dialogue sessions between Blacks and Whites on the Southwest side. Everyone recognized the critical need but only Carmen and I were willing to commit time to it at that point. Naturally, we both immediately thought Bill Creed would be an asset to our planning and would also be able to provide people to participate from his parish.

Carmen called him and he eagerly embraced the idea. He had experienced so much pain and mistrust when he began his pastorate at St. Hiltrudis. He arrived there on the eve of the great White exodus to the suburbs. He suffered when parishioners left, some in the dark of night, without a word of farewell. He pleaded with them from the pulpit to at least say good-bye.

The parish was in turmoil, and he was desperate for some way to break the pattern so familiar in changing neighborhoods. He felt strongly that any attempts to improve the quality of relationships between the Races were consequential. He knew the Blacks who moved into the parish felt pain and rejection. It was a difficult time.

Bill invited several parishioners, and Carmen and I invited four White women who agreed to participate. Unfortunately, we were unable to convince some of the persons we knew struggled with their racism, but we had to begin somewhere. The meeting began with some awkwardness and obvious discomfort. As each of us introduced ourselves, we learned a bit about the experiences of each other. The Blacks who came with Father Creed admitted they would not have driven to the meeting site had he not been driving, generating an obvious response of discomfort from the White women who shifted their weight and grimaced slightly.

One Black woman in her late thirties began the conversation.

"I remember being terribly frightened the first Sunday I drove to Mass at St. Hiltrudis and saw the crowd of people standing on the front sidewalk. As we drew closer, my husband, two children and I discussed whether we would even get out of the vehicle. Then the eggs came splattering across the windshield, the hood, the doors, and windows on the left side. My children cried in fear as they ducked between the seats, and my husband stepped on the gas to get us out of harm's way as soon as possible. We went home trembling and angry. We thought we moved to a better and safer neighborhood."

"We never even tried to go to Mass for several months," said a father of four. "We missed the Eucharist but were too frightened to even think about going. It was only when Father Creed personally called and invited us to participate that we agreed to try. He told us he and some other members of the parish would greet us at the front entrance and forestall hostile demonstrations. In fact he made arrangements with the local police department to have uniformed personnel present at the doors of Church for the Sunday liturgies."

"We never expected that kind of response. I guess we were naive. We're a little older now and hoped to retire in a nice neighborhood," added a recently-retired gentleman. "If it hadn't been for Father Creed and a few of our neighbors, some of whom are White, we would have fled the day after we arrived."

Finally, one of the White women from the suburb spoke timidly and haltingly. "I know I can't speak for Whites, but I apologize for what some have done to you. We are not all like that. We moved to the suburbs, not because of people like you, but because some Blacks and Whites are so destructive and violent. We feared for the safety of our children and ourselves."

"I just don't know the answer. I guess nobody has it. It's a known fact that property values go down when a neighborhood changes. How possible is it to truly have integration?"

There was no question that we tackled a difficult issue, and I recalled my own experiences in the fifties with Friendship House gatherings. It seemed hopeless, but the folks at the meeting agreed to come again.

During this same period of time, the city of Chicago initiated a busing plan, which would transport students from over-crowded elementary schools to other underutilized area schools which were under-utilized. For the most part, this meant Black students would travel by bus, sometimes long distances, to schools in mostly white areas. The rage and outcry throughout part of the city was a disgrace.

One of the schools affected was in the neighborhood in which the Provincial House was located. It was very difficult and upsetting to watch the evening news and see the terror on the faces of the young Black students when greeted by jeering and shouts from the crowd gathered at the school entrance. After two or three of these evenings, I felt compelled to ask for some sort of expression of support for the busing proposal from the Province Team.

Brigid suggested we draft a proposal for the Chapter and affirm our support of equal opportunity for all. That didn't surprise me because she was always somewhat reluctant to make a statement that would generate opposition.

Louise Ann offered, "We could do that, but the Chapter doesn't meet for several months. I think we need to do something now."

Carmen, usually simple and direct, offered, "How about standing at the bus stop when the children arrive and smiling and waving to them. At least they'll see a few friendly faces in the crowd."

That seemed to satisfy the team members who feared we had become too political already, and gave an outlet to those who feared we would appear apathetic to this critical situation in our own back yard. So, for the next several days, several of us stood as a welcoming committee in a forest of adversaries. We simply stood there as the bus arrived, saying nothing, but smiling and waving as the youngsters arrived. The shouting was so loud in opposition to their presence that we knew any words would be futile. It seemed terribly inconsequential, but we felt the open hostility they experienced would scar the young children.

Soon after our tactic was perceived by the crowd, we were verbally attacked by many of those who harassed the children.

"Who are you and where do you come from?"

"Do you belong in this neighborhood? Who sent you?"

Finally, one of the group recognized Mary, her high-school religion teacher.

"Sister Mary, what are you doing here? Don't you understand what this is all about? How could you do this to us?"

Before she could respond, a group close by heard "Sister Mary" and gathered closer around us menacingly.

"Are all of you nuns?"

"Yes, we are. We are Sisters of Hope. We all work at the Provincial House just a few blocks away."

"Sisters of Hope! We all graduated from Mother Mary High School. We would expect you to support us in this. Our homes are at stake."

We tried to give some explanation for our presence, but they would hear none of it.

"We don't want to hurt the children, but the City Council has failed us and now it looks like the Sisters have turned us off as well."

By now, the children were safely in the school and the crowd began to disperse, shaking their heads and muttering to one another about being let down by the Church. In fact, the Church *had* let them down, and so had we.

CHAPTER SEVENTEEN

The turmoil and conflict in society was paralleled by minor chaos within the structures of the Catholic Church, much of it around priestly celibacy. A growing number of priests left priesthood for the purpose of marrying. Some were engaged in sexual relationships when they left and became fathers shortly. Others not pushed to the choice by pregnancy, believed their love relationship was far more valuable than the life of celibacy. Others continued in their priesthood even though they had already crossed the line in terms of heterosexual relationships.

Conversations, articles and meetings explored the possibility of returning to a time before celibacy and priesthood were merged. Large groups of priests and others advocated a return to early Christianity where celibacy was not mandatory for ordination. The expectation was that in a short time this would change. Clearly, this had implications for the role of women in the Church. Priests must be "pure," and never touch a woman. Women must be banned from the sanctuary. The coalescence of groups advocating optional celibacy and ordination of women generated a cauldron of hearty debate.

Surveys among Catholics revealed a growing readiness for married clergy and the beginning of ground support for women priests. It all looked so positive and hopeful, but it was no less impossible than achieving racial equality. However, within this ambience of projection and anticipation, many relationships between priests and women continued to develop.

Bill and I rejoiced in the prospects that the time might come when we could marry and continue in ministry. I knew that would have implications for my membership in a religious community, but I felt the ministry was more important and welcomed the dreams that were generated by considering Bill and I ministering together as a married couple.

We were aware of our deepening friendship developing a strong desire, albeit need, to express our love beyond kissing and hugging. We talked long hours about what was happening to each of us. Even if things changed, we knew, we were still held by the bonds of our commitments. At times, the sexual attraction diminished as we considered our strong desire to respond to our calls.

Bill began to share his feelings more freely than he ever had.

"Marsha, I've never felt this way before. I can't imagine myself living without you in my life. At times I am scared about where this could lead. I'm selfish, I know, but I don't want to do anything to hurt you or jeopardize the respect and affection so many in your community and beyond have for you. I become depressed and unhappy when I think about a future without you. At the same time, I know I can't give up priesthood. I wouldn't know who I was, and it would be so disappointing to my family and others. I feel so alive and so loved with you. This can't be wrong."

"I feel very much the same, Bill. I'm more caring and sensitive. You have softened some of my hard edges and I like that. I bring you to prayer and find that very peaceful. I feel at times that God has given us each other so that we can continue on our course. I was drained and disenchanted when we first began to know each other, as you know."

We were both disillusioned with church and religious life structures. The energy and passion we found in them before no longer contributed to our effectiveness in ministry. We were depleted in many respects and lost the zeal that once energized us. We seemed to face resistance to our goals and dreams from the very people with whom we worked. Perhaps we could reconnect with some of that passion if we worked together in ministry.

Bill acknowledged his frustration with the reluctance of members of his staff to move in new directions. He felt shackled with an associate priest who was young and recently ordained. He seemed threatened by Bill's attempt to incorporate lay persons in more significant roles in the parish. He opposed many of the changes Bill proposed. He wanted to keep things the same. People were not ready for changes.

"Marsha, I'm feeling burnt out here. I can't seem to get anything going. I feel like I'm wasting my time. The people deserve better and I can't seem to pull it off," Bill shared in one of our heart-to-heart talks. He added, "You're the reason I keep going at this. I feel you understand and support me more than anyone else. When we talk, I get fired up about what could happen here, but when I come back, I feel helpless to do anything about it."

I was feeling frustrated, too. My vision and goals, shared with the province at the onset of my administration, were no longer valued by many of the members of my religious community. Apparently I was moving too far and too fast. My attempts to engage the Order in confronting systemic evils of sexism, racism and poverty often resulted in an impasse at community meetings. It seemed my leadership style was no longer what many of the larger community members wanted or valued.

We began to collaborate on programs in the parish where Bill was pastor. Those led us more and more to realize that we worked well together. It seemed wonderful for us and others to have the opportunity to participate in activities and programs that were facilitated by a man and a woman on topics like spirituality, justice and worship. The male presence was so predominant within the church that many had little or no exposure to women in public ministry, much less male and female collaboration. Our experimentation with working together and the kind of reception we received encouraged us to continue to model new ways of ministry.

There was a new role beginning to develop in the Archdiocese at that point, one that involved the presence of women as members of pastoral teams which heretofore had been composed of priests and male deacons. The role of Pastoral Associate was designed to create opportunities for women to have greater visibility in parish ministry and to involve them in shaping the direction in which the parish would grow. It was in its infancy but it opened up possibilities for me to continue ministry in a parish setting. That was, in fact, what I had hoped to do when I was so unexpectedly elected to serve as Provincial. My term was almost up and I knew I would not leave my name available for another term, nor did I think I would even be asked to consider such a thing.

With all of this going on, Bill and I sought and found solace in each other's presence. When we felt misunderstood or unappreciated, we found support and healing with each other. The struggle to maintain our relationship on an even keel, within the limits of the Church, confronted the growing desire we each experienced for greater intimacy. It was only a matter of time before our desires would override the restraints of the institutions with which each of us was becoming more disenchanted.

We were not disillusioned about our calls, however, and firmly believed our friendship was a gift from God, leading us to a renewed commitment to our call to continue to build the kingdom of God in a renewed Church. Our attempts to discern God's will for our relationship in prayer, spiritual direction and retreats led us to the conviction that God was very much in this relationship. Never did anyone suggest in our retreats that we abandon each other. We were always encouraged to accept it as gift and continue to stay the course.

But our growing and deepening love for each other continued to make demands on us for greater intimacy. One day, Bill shared the difficulty he was experiencing as a result of our physical closeness. "Marsha, at times when we are together, I find myself getting very excited. I appreciate that we are trying to stay within the limits of our commitments, but I often feel physical discomfort after we have been together with passionate embraces."

I truly was not aware of what he meant. That kind of closeness with a man was foreign. While I certainly yearned for a deeper intimacy, I continued to believe we should not be engaged in anything more. Sometimes, I was even uncomfortable with the closeness we shared, but so far, nothing had happened. I offered a response to his comment. "Bill, I love the closeness and feel a desire for more. Maybe we should try to return to the way we were in the beginning. Do you want to try?"

"Marsha, I don't think there is any way to turn back. I have never felt more like a man than I do now. I know our love has been the stimulus and impetus for renewing my energy in ministry. I have to believe this is what God is doing in my life."

Clearly, though, our deepening love was leading to increased desire for more and was becoming a concern for each of us, but we felt as long as we maintained the restraints on our expression of love, we would be okay. The question, though, was for how much longer we could continue to do that and how willing we were to forego what we both longed for. Whenever we concluded our time together and held to our goals, we were relieved, proud, but increasingly unsettled.

The first time we spent a night in the same place happened quite by chance. Bill had arranged to use a friend's house in the country for the day. It was always such a problem to find time alone, where we would not likely meet anyone who knew us. There was always an air of secrecy that needed to surround our relationship and that was extremely stressful. I hated sneaking around and firmly believed we did not have to apologize to anyone because we had done nothing wrong.

When Bill picked me up, he asked. "Do you feel up for a ride?'

"When I'm with you, I'm up for just about anything. I've really been looking forward to spending this day with you. Where are we going?"

"Bass Lake. I have the keys to my classmate's house for the day. I thought we could play tennis at the courts near there, have lunch, and enjoy the afternoon near the water. It's right on the lake and could be a nice day for us. Would that be okay with you?"

"Sounds great to me! You really are full of surprises."

When we arrived, we played tennis, enjoyed lunch at a nearby café, and then purchased some food for supper. I thought it might be nice to have dinner in a homey setting. It was so much more natural, and it would be fun to finally have dinner alone. The evening turned quite cool so Bill started a fire, and we set a small table in front of it for dinner. It was very romantic, actually, and we both enjoyed our food and conversation.

As we ate, a ferocious storm blew up, a mid-western gale with crashing rolls of thunder, lightening that lit up the darkened room, and hail that pelted windows and roof with a vengeance. This type of storm is usually short-term, but this one did not show signs of abating any time soon. In fact, the weather forecaster advised persons to stay off the roads unless it was absolutely necessary.

We waited a few more hours and decided it was foolish to try to make the return trip that evening. We called our respective residences and explained our absence. The sisters with whom I lived knew I was with Bill, but I know the priest he lived with was not aware of that. We prepared a bed for each of us in separate rooms.

The tension was palpable, each of us wanting to share the same bed, but also very much aware that we wanted to do nothing that would compromise the other. The raging of the storm and the howling of the winds were nothing compared to the turmoil I was feeling. I assumed Bill was very much in the same place as he held me in his arms for the last time that evening.

"Bill, did you ever think we would be this closely involved when we first became friends?"

"Not really, I just thought we would laugh and eat out a lot."

As we parted to go to our respective rooms, we struggled to let go of each other, feeling the excitement of our closeness and desperately wanting to conclude this day together in complete physical intimacy. It was definitely what each of us longed for, but afraid to take the next step, we parted to endure a restless and agonizing night apart.

The next morning we departed very early, with Bill hoping to make it back in time for the celebration of liturgy at the convent. He had arranged with his associate to do that in case he was late. He was not more than a minute late, but Jeff had already begun the Mass.

He called later that morning to inquire about my reception when I returned home.

"How was Lydia? Did she have any comments or give you one of her judgmental looks?"

"No, but I don't think she liked it and suspected more went on with us than actually did. She has little room to comment, though, as she and Barry are very close, too. She has stayed overnight with him many times. I never question what they do or how they carry on when they are away."

The experience of that night disturbed us both, and we realized how close we came to moving beyond where either of us wanted to go. We wanted to remain faithful to our commitments. We carefully avoided talking about it for a while so as not to open a new dimension of conflict. Our struggles often minimized the joy of our love. For the next several times we met, we were very much more reserved in our affectionate responses. We tried to reassure ourselves that we could do this; this was God's will for us. We could be very close friends and not end up in bed, like several other priests and nuns we knew.

Our commitment to each other became a defining one for each of us and set us on a journey that involved many agonizing probes, reflections, soul-searching, and resolutions. Our resolve was to cherish our love but make it consistent with our other commitments. We were rarely able to sustain that for long. We had become soul-mates, but we were also lovers, friends and ministers. Each of us was held by the restraints of church and family, and it was impossible to consider a lifestyle change.

Yet, we were impelled by the power and energy of our love. At some point, it became clear to us that the question about whether or not we would continue in our relationship was not negotiable. We were committed to each other, and we would try to live that in ways consistent with our calls. We made no secret of the fact that we were close friends. My family was aware of our friendship and welcomed Bill wholeheartedly. They knew how important we had become to each other, but we never talked about all the dimensions of our physical expression. Bill's family members, however, refused to accept the fact that we were even friends. That was often a source of tension between Bill and me. His sisters could not even entertain the possibility that their priest-brother would have a close woman friend. We firmly believed our love relationship was making us more effective in our ministries. We both saw this prohibition around sexual expression as archaic and totally irresponsible. We were deeply spiritual persons, committed to ministry and service, and we loved each other. The requirement of celibacy was part of a larger issue for the Church—the nature of woman and her role in the scheme of life and church. While the Church was unwilling to confront this, we lived with the hope that someday that conversation would happen and changes would follow.

CHAPTER EIGHTEEN

The issue regarding women and their role in ministry was a burning one for me, and we dealt with it directly and indirectly very often. I firmly believed that women belonged in the priesthood. In fact, we allowed and encouraged several of our members who felt this call to pursue the studies that prepared for this full expression of ministry. Two or three of them shared with me the struggles they experienced as they confronted the sexist structures of the Church even in their studies.

I did not know this was the issue on Mary's mind when she walked into my office one morning with a more resolute determination than usual. She smiled as she crossed from the door to stand in front of my desk, and I knew whatever was on her mind would involve me. Mary was a remarkably energetic and effective member of the Team. Her creative projects and innovations in elementary education had been responsible for dramatic changes in the curriculum and functioning of some of the schools our Order sponsored.

"Marsha, I checked with your secretary. You have no scheduled appointments today. There's something I've wanted to do for quite some time and this might be the perfect day. Come on with me. You are important to this." She gave me one of her looks that brokered no opposition.

I was not normally so compliant, but she was a trusted friend, and I was glad to have an opportunity to spend some time away from the office. The prolonged struggle over the elderly housing proposal had taken a toll on my enthusiasm for the role and the possibilities for influencing change. One of my primary goals in accepting the position was to lead us to a more visible and viable presence for justice.

Carmen, the Assistant Provincial, recently resigned citing some of the same reasons. I was reprimanded by some of the community members for allowing that to happen. I should have insisted she complete her term, I was told. I still had one more year to serve and I would complete it, but I was aware that something was changing for me in terms of job satisfaction. I no longer looked forward to coming into the office. Business at hand was much more administrative and internal to the Order, much like it had been in Maryland, and it was draining my enthusiasm.

The zeal and excitement with which I began my term as provincial was powerful. The eagerness of many members for a justice thrust was still present, but there was a growing erosion of that as the issues began to generate the inevitable controversy such commitments sparked. I questioned myself and my ability to lead this group. What right did I have to disrupt their lives and perhaps even tarnish the image of the Order in the Chicago area?

Today could be a pleasant break in the routine. The weather was sunny and pleasant, an early tease of spring. "Okay, Mary, I place myself in your hands. Let's go," I said as I placed my arm around her shoulder.

We were not on the road very long before she gave me some

inkling of what she had in mind. "I want to do some shopping and I need you to help with the selection."

I turned toward her with a puzzled expression. She was one of the members of the team whose clothes reflected the simplicity of her life style. She was surely not taking me on a shopping binge for clothing. She picked up on my expression and smiled. "There are a few things I think we ought to consider purchasing for the province."

"What are you talking about?"

"You'll see."

We parked in the shopping area lot and proceeded to a counter in one of the large department stores. There were a number of pewter wine goblets and small plates on display. The symbolism was not lost on me. These were often used by the clergy for celebrating Eucharist when they did not want to use the golden chalices inlaid with their mother's diamond. This was typically the gift given to priests at their ordination.

As we fingered the items, she said, "I thought it would be supportive if we gave the three women who have been preparing for ordination these symbols of our affirmation and confirmation of their call. It would probably be a good idea to include Caroline since she will be starting her program in the fall. You know how discouraged they become and how frustrated they are when they see their male classmates move through the same program of studies as they do but continue on to ordination. I know we can't change that rule, but I thought we might at least let them know we are aware of their pain," she said.

"I like it, but I wonder how this will be received. You know how skeptical I have become about making any gestures or statements on controversial issues. I'm not sure the province will endorse this action." Once again, I felt the reluctance that was becoming more characteristic of my response to issues of justice. I felt the disillusionment erupting in me.

"I wasn't thinking of a big public presentation, just a gathering of the Province Team and the four women involved. It would be a vote of confidence for them if they shared their experience with us. At the conclusion of that sharing, we could have a simple ritual and present them with the chalice and plates, confirming our belief in their call to priesthood," she said.

We purchased four chalices and plates and made arrangements to have them inscribed. We then took a leisurely ride to a quaint country inn for lunch. While we ate, we decided how we would share our plan with the team at the next meeting. Then we spent the rest of the time catching up on each other's personal lives.

"How are things with you and Bill?" she asked. She and I talked many times about our developing friendship but it had been a while.

"Fine, on one hand. We are very good friends and good for each other. We accomplish so much when we work together. It is a struggle, though, and at times I'm confused and conflicted with the depth of our feelings and the closeness we experience. At times I feel able to pull it off, at other times, the intensity of our love makes me feel the best thing we can do is to separate from each other," I said with tears in my eyes. Tears were becoming very common for me now.

"I'd hate to see that happen, Marsha. I've seen how alive and energetic you are with him, and I know how trying this province role has become. I'd be concerned if you didn't have Bill in your life. Don't be so hard on yourself. You're only human and you've been through a lot this past couple of years. Continue to share your life with him. I know how much he needs you as well."

We didn't pursue that subject any further. There really was no easy solution. It meant a lot to me that she was aware of where I was coming from and was eager to support me in the relationship. As we left the inn, she hugged me and told me, "Hang in there. He's a good man, and you're a good woman."

I knew hers was a minority opinion; others took a different line, questioning our relationship and judging us harshly. Bill, who had been one of the priests most often called on to celebrate liturgies for special community events, was seldom invited any more. Rumors and innuendos ran rampant in some circles, making us both very uncomfortable. That was another reason for my unwillingness to stay on as Provincial. It was a very high profile position and many expected absolute adherence to the rules. The irony was that Bill and I had not been unfaithful to that point.

In any case, Mary and I went ahead with our plans for the meeting with the women who pursued studies toward ordination. The three women presently enrolled in the theological schools shared their convictions about being called to priesthood, the exhilaration they felt in practicing the rituals associated with ordination, and the resulting pain they experienced in being denied full access to ordained ministry.

"I get so angry at some of the men with whom I have been in class these three years," said Alyssa, the youngest of the group who had been forthright about her call to ordained ministry from the time she first entered the Order. "As they approach the date for their ordination they are filled with themselves and seem to have no sensitivity to what I might be feeling at being excluded. When I try to talk with them, I feel put down and they remind me I should have known I wouldn't be ordained when I began the program."

"Even the guys who do want to be supportive feel the constraints of the system. They don't want to become too vocal for fear it will jeopardize their own ordination," said Ruth Mary. "It's such a disappointment to feel included in everything up to now and then be excluded from the final step because I'm a woman."

Thomas Ann, the most recent person to enter a theological program, chose a seminary that was quite different from the one the others attended. It was inter-denominational and did not require that she live on the campus. As a result, her ties to the other seminarians were less intimate. For the moment, she was enjoying the interaction with the men and women who represented a diverse religious background. However, she added she fully expected to feel the frustration of Alyssa and Ruth Mary as she moved closer to the completion of her studies.

After a bit more conversation, I moved toward the celebration of ritual and presentation of gifts. "We're here tonight because all of us have been aware of your pain and wanted to offer some symbol of our continued support. We're struggling, too, as we search for ways we might impact this intransigent institution."

Mary then presented each of the four with the chalice and plate engraved with their names and the date. Tears welled in their eyes as they took the gift and saw their name and "Called to Ordination—October, 1978." It was a powerful experience for all of us. We concluded with a celebration of bread and wine, a foreshadowing of what we hoped would become a reality in the near future.

As the women left, clutching their gifts, they were effusive in their expression of gratitude. This was truly a moment on their journey, which would continue to energize them to continue the course. Their leadership team was right there with them.

Upon further reflection on that meeting, I felt it was necessary to take one more step. I was generally unable to walk away from injustice without making some statement or taking some action. I said to the team members, "We need to do more than privately acknowledge and affirm the call of some women to ordination. There is too much of that operating in the clergy and hierarchy already. They speak words of support and encouragement for the ordination of women, but their public stance echoes the official Church position."

I talked with Bill about this as well, sharing my frustration and the need to take the discussion to another level. He was supportive but cautious, reluctant to have me take on another cause that might only result in further disappointment. The defeat of the elderly housing project and the school busing travesty and the resulting dissension within the province had taken its toll, but I felt ready for one more effort toward the development of a more equitable role for women in the Church.

CHAPTER NINETEEN

The strategy we developed began when I contacted the President and Vice-President of Academic Affairs at the theological school. At the first meeting, they encouraged my pursuit of this issue and expressed their willingness to cooperate. They would provide the necessary documentation to certify that Alyssa had successfully completed all the educational requirements for ordination. This was the first step in the process that male students took toward becoming ordained.

The next step involved soliciting letters from persons whom she ministered to in order to ascertain her credibility and effectiveness in ministry. Our request for those letters netted almost a hundred responses. They came from members of our community, priests with whom she interacted in ministry and a number of lay people who benefited from her ministry.

The third and final step in the process was to present the candidate for ordination to the Bishop for his decision. It is the Bishop who calls a person to ordination; in our case, it was Cardinal Carey. When I called him for an appointment, he responded immediately, never asking what it was I wished to discuss. I wasn't sure whether that was a good or a bad thing.

With the necessary documentation, I arrived at his residence with Alyssa. I was very nervous as I waited for the door to open. I was anxious about this meeting. The Cardinal was not known for his sensitivity or gentleness in dealing with people, but my previous experiences with him had given me a little confidence that he was kinder in one-on-one settings than in the public forum.

I was shocked when the door opened and the Cardinal himself filled the open frame. I expected someone else on door duty; I needed to go to the bathroom. The ride and the anticipation of the meeting had taken a toll on my kidneys and bladder.

"Good morning, Sisters. I'm all alone here this morning. Come in."

"Good morning, Your Eminence. We really appreciate your seeing us on Saturday. I'd like you to meet Sister Alyssa."

He greeted her and began to move from the foyer when I asked, "Is there a rest room convenient, Cardinal?" I knew I'd never last through a meeting, even if it ended rather abruptly and suddenly.

"Sure. Right over here." He led me to a brown door down the hall and excused himself saying he would return shortly. I entered the washroom quickly, leaving Alyssa standing alone in the lobby. When I emerged, she was grinning, apparently at my first words to the Cardinal.

When the Cardinal returned he led us to a luxurious parlor, filled with large antique chairs, some tables and lamps of a rare vintage, and huge stained glass windows. The figures in the windows were all male, bishops or priests from the early days of the Church. Voluminous maroon velvet drapes hung on both sides of the eight windows. The room was dimly-lit and colorless. The Cardinal turned on a lamp near the chair he selected for himself. As he settled into the largest seat in the room, he directed us to two smaller velvet chairs across a small coffee table from him. No appointments softened the room, only some books, a Bible and other religious artifacts. Presumably, they told a story, but that wasn't why we were here.

"I know why you're here, Sister," the Cardinal began "It's about Prince of Peace Retirement Home, isn't it?"

"No, Cardinal, I wasn't aware of a reason to discuss that. I'm here to talk about the ordination of women."

His head jerked abruptly and he sputtered, "But…that's not permitted."

"Yes, I know, but I thought it might be good to begin some conversation about it. I asked Alyssa to join us because she will be completing the course of studies from the Donum Dei Seminary in a couple of months. With the support of the administration, we have all the necessary documentation and wanted to take this final step of presenting her to you."

With the mention of Donum Dei, a recent site of protests from women during some of their ceremonies, he looked at Alyssa. "Have you been involved in any of those demonstrations there? I don't understand how they can do that at a sacred service. Did you participate in those disruptions?"

"I stood in silent protest, but that is all I did," she responded.

"You nuns have got to stop trying to make things happen your way. The Church has spoken and you should just obey and stop the protests. Why is it so important that you be ordained? Is there something lacking in your ministry because you cannot be a priest?"

"Yes, Cardinal Carey, there is." She spoke eloquently about the frustration of walking with people as they journey to healing, forgiveness, marriage, etc. but then having to bring them to a priest to have the sacraments administered. She described very convincingly, I thought, her pain at being excluded from celebrating the mysteries because she was a woman. She told him how effective she was in the classes; how much her classmates admired and supported her and appreciated her insights and contributions. She told of her anger when they prepared to celebrate their reception of the various orders that led to ordination, and they urged her not to disrupt their big day. The Cardinal seemed to listen but eventually told her to do the best she could with the ministry available to her. He then rambled, as lonely men are wont to do. He described at length a friendship he had with a nun in his previous diocese. He appreciated the gifts of his female friends but believed Rome was right in denying ordination to women. "After all, if Jesus had wanted to have women priests, he would have ordained them himself."

"He didn't even ordain men. He called persons to follow him closely and they were women as well as men," Alyssa blurted.

"Oh, but he did ordain men, Sister Alyssa, at the Last Supper."

"Recent research indicates that was not what Jesus intended, and there were women at the Last Supper."

This was going nowhere so I looked for an opportunity to end the conversation. "It was good of you to hear us, Cardinal. We only wanted to initiate a dialogue. We did not expect that anything would change as a result of our visit."

"It can't, Sister, because that is how God wants it."

Alyssa and I collapsed into the car, relieved that the meeting was over and we had made our points. We were eager to head home. Our friends waited for each of us, anxious to hear the outcome. We never expected any change as a result of the meeting, but there was one more phase to accomplish before we put the matter to rest.

I drafted a letter to the almost two hundred fifty bishops throughout the country in which I described the cordial meeting with Cardinal Carey about the possibility of ordination of women. I acknowledged that he clearly reaffirmed the official Church position prohibiting that. However, I wanted them to know we were eager to explore this with any of them who might be interested in pursuing a dialogue on the subject.

Only five bishops even acknowledged receipt of the letter and one invited further discussion. He was from a southern diocese and suggested a meeting with him if I visited his area. It was not something I wished to pursue. I learned that Cardinal Carey was quite upset that I referred to the meeting as 'cordial.' He told one of the priests close to the Chancery, "That meeting should never have happened. We are not even supposed to talk about ordination of women."

When our Chapter convened, we explained the process we undertook and invited the delegates to respond to the proposed resolution supporting ordination of women. I was once again flattened by the outcry of resistance to our action. I presented the resolution as an issue of equality, one that was consistent with the thrust of our province team. Some Chapter delegates adamantly denied us the right to take any action relative to that issue. We had no business questioning the Church's authority. Still others criticized us for even considering it a matter of justice.

The unwillingness of the Chapter to support this action was difficult enough; the negative criticism by a large number of Sisters for even addressing the issue really hurt. Letters and phone calls supporting my action were few and dulled by the deluge of objections.

My term was drawing to a close and I was very grateful. These three years had taken a toll on me and it seemed to accelerate. I presided over the Chapter of Elections six weeks later and listened to the description of the kind of person the delegates preferred for the next provincial. Some things sounded familiar to me, but there was a strong expression of caution about taking stands. The general consensus was to return to a style of leadership that was more docile toward the institutional Church. The sisters did not want to be embarrassed by public stands, especially where the hierarchy was concerned.

I had no regrets about the terms of my service, but it was now clear that my usefulness to the province was ended. The final crushing blow came after I passed by a group during a recess in the Chapter. The condemnatory tirade was led by my mentor in high school. As she expounded her venomous comment, someone indicated to her that I was passing by. She ceased immediately and turned to me, smiling. "I love you, Marsha, but I hate what you're doing."

I was spiritless as I went through the motions during that Chapter. By now I was eager to leave all the chaos, ready to move on to new ministry. Bill invited me to serve as pastoral associate at his parish. I was delighted to have the opportunity to work with him and serve the parish. In a matter of weeks the provincial role would be finished, but I was not.

CHAPTER TWENTY

While it was true I was not finished or wiped out, I was significantly diminished in my energy and enthusiasm. I planned a retreat when I completed the term, and I followed through with that plan. I found a tremendous resource in Scriptural prayer. My personal relationship with Jesus continued to motivate me and allowed me to link my rejection and suffering to His. There was considerable comfort in that for me at that time. The spirituality that drove me during those years was conformity to the passion, death and resurrection model of Jesus. There seemed little of resurrection just now, but it would return.

Upon completion of the retreat, which provided rest as well as prayer and direction, I began to develop a role in the parish. It was a new position and my creative energies were limited but I enjoyed making the effort. I was disappointed with the way my term ended and angry, too, that I had been duped in some ways to accept the nomination to that election. I was floundering for a renewed sense of call. I questioned myself and wondered if I was unfaithful to the call. Was Bill an obstacle to my being an effective minister?

That question was one that dominated the retreat. The resounding support I received from the person who directed me during that time was reassuring. He told me Bill was a special gift, one that enabled me to undertake the difficult tasks of confronting injustice. He strongly encouraged me to continue in that relationship. It was life-giving for him and for me. The Church was changing and there would come a time when this kind of relationship would be the norm for ministers.

While there was not open support for this kind of relationship when it led to greater physical intimacy, it was assumed by many spiritual directors that there were lapses. After all, they would say, most members of the clergy and religious communities entered with a very poorly developed sense of their own sexuality. Many had never experienced being in love. If there are lapses, be gentle with yourselves and renew your commitments to celibacy. It will be a struggle, I was reminded, but keep on trying.

Bill and I relished the opportunity to work together and to see each other almost every day. We both felt renewed in spirit. He finally had a companion who shared his dreams and goals for the parish. I welcomed the opportunities available to me to preach on a regular basis, to prepare persons to receive the sacraments, to minister to the sick and dying, and to model a new style of ministry. People seemed to welcome the feminine input into programs and planning. The parish seemed to come alive. For the moment, my conflicts with the institutional Church were minimized. Opportunities to preach necessitated a more concentrated reflection on Scripture so that my words would reflect the meaning and purpose of the passages read each Sunday.

I responded to a growing number of invitations to give retreats and days of reflection in other settings. I was recognized as one with a gift that women eagerly longed for. I began to develop Women's Spirituality Seminars and spent many hours with groups of women in several parishes. I began to feel restored; my disappointments with province leadership dissipated. Here was my call now. I needed a broader population. The other staff members welcomed me and were happy for a new voice, as well. They struggled, too. Being White ministers in a predominantly Black community had its down side, especially as Blacks discovered their own sense of identity. Most of the people were gracious, but hesitant to commit totally to what we were trying to develop. There was not unanimous agreement among the parishioners either. When some sought to develop a choir that was more inspirational for them, others decried it as a "return to Baptist religion."

"I left the Baptist Church because of that music. It's so loud and much too lively for the Catholic Church."

"Why are you giving in to those people? They ought to go back to what they left."

There was lots of turmoil, eventually, as the people became more involved in shaping the decisions and direction for the parish. The school was really more important to many of the families than the Church. It offered a viable alternative to what was available through the local public schools. Even those who were not Catholic wanted their children taught in an environment that provided safety, discipline and a sense of values. There was a much greater participation in school-related activities than in church events. It was frustrating for me as most of my preparation and orientation was toward adults. When we advertised some sort of personal growth opportunities, the turn-out was minimal or non-existent.

We continued to plan, hoping things would change in time, but in the meantime I was getting impatient with the slowness of development. I took on other commitments; peace and justice groups formed throughout the Archdiocese; women's groups developed to create more opportunities for women to be involved in Church planning and decision making. I continued to minister at the parish but sought out other experiences so that I would not feel totally ineffective.

At the same time, Bill and I were deepening our love while being very circumspect in the parish. People knew and accepted our friendship, but we were reluctant to push the limits publicly. So the secrecy of our closeness continued until one day the inevitable happened— we celebrated our love in complete intimacy. It was wonderful to experience being loved so totally and completely by another person. Each of us was overwhelmed with the joy and delight and love that filled our souls. Neither of us had such an experience before. We were ecstatic for the moment.

Within a very short time, each of us experienced guilt and anxiety. We had transgressed our vows, and we each rushed to Confession so that we could be at peace once again. That same cycle continued for some time--intimacy followed by confession, confusion and anger. Neither of us ever expected this to happen and yet we acknowledged that our relationship and the needs for greater closeness were inevitable.

I knew we were not alone in our situation. I counseled others, sisters as well as priests, who engaged in genital intimacy. The women would talk with one another about the experience and the struggle. The priests would never acknowledge to another priest, even their closest friends, that they were having this kind of relationship.

Tension began to escalate between Bill and me. I felt this passionate love that we shared was a call from God to challenge the structures. I believed if more of the persons involved in such relationships went public, perhaps the hierarchy would see that celibacy was not working for many clergy. Bill somehow managed to incorporate this into his life and reaffirmed his position that he could never leave priesthood.

"I told you from the beginning I was selfish, Marsha, and this is what I meant. I have compromised you and yet I love you so much that I want to continue in relationship with you. I can't leave to marry. I would not know who I was if not a priest. Eventually, I would resent you."

"That's absurd, Bill. You speak of yourself as priest as though that were your real and only identity. Priesthood is a role and does not create an ontological change in your person."

That went nowhere and we continued to struggle with what was happening. I could not live with myself and continue in that kind of relationship, yet, I was unwilling to forego the joys of knowing love like ours. The physical intimacy would have to stop. To facilitate that, I made the decision to move to another ministry in a different location. We would try to maintain our friendship but diminish the full effect of our passion for each other.

I felt tremendous conflict within and considered the possibility of leaving religious life. This was becoming too difficult, but I didn't see myself returning to the lifestyle I embraced those many years ago. Even if Bill would not make a change, I would in order to keep myself more honest. I, too, was afraid of the implications of that change and the effect it would have on families and friends. I couldn't make the decision yet, but I could feel myself withdrawing more and more from religious community on a daily basis. I lived alone now and participated very little in province events. I knew I was distancing myself, and I fully expected it would just be a temporary phase.

Each of us continued in spiritual direction and even began psychological counseling so that we might better understand how to cope with the reality of our lives. I experienced depression and knew it was my anger focused inward. I was angry with myself for having been unfaithful. I was angry with Bill for being unwilling to consider marriage. I was angry with the Church for its intransigence around issues of celibacy and women in ministry. When the anger became too much to bear, I succumbed to depression, which definitely affected my ministry choices the next several years after I left the parish.

Bill and I tried to temper our passions. We spent much less time together, called each other less frequently, and became increasingly miserable. He was persuasive in convincing me we could resume our friendship and stay within the boundaries. I desperately wanted to believe that was true as I had been incredibly lonely, too. We prayed together, sought counseling together and tried to cope with the struggle for celibate friendship.

My ministry change brought me into a new experience that was at once challenging and frustrating. There was a group of people forming an organization intent on bringing to light some of the issues of injustice present in the Church. It was a wonderful group of people who had a vision I shared and hoped to bring to some concrete expression. The leader of the group was a former priest, married to a woman who was an advocate for change as well. I think I was just too tired to become involved in a new project that required more of me than I had available at that time. After two years, I resigned from the organization.

Once more, I needed to search again for a ministry where I might hopefully regain a sense of involvement with my religious community. One of our sisters approached me to assist in a very innovative project. It would require me to recruit and train people to serve as house parents for a new development. It would offer an alternative setting for persons who were mentally and physically challenged.

CHAPTER TWENTY-ONE

In the meantime, Bill was in his own transition. Shortly after I left St. Hiltrudis, he was contacted by the Priest Personnel Board to consider accepting a pastorate in an affluent White suburb. He was told none of the priests who applied for that position in Bluff Lakes seemed appropriate. The Board wanted him for the job. None of them was aware of how drained he was.

In fact, some of my friends in the Order and I tried to convince Bill to take some time away for retooling or renewing or whatever. He had worked so hard for more than thirty years—often accepting assignments to very difficult parish and/or rectory situations—at the whim of the personnel placement people. They knew he was a very generous and gracious priest who would make every attempt to work things out no matter how difficult the circumstances. He was placed in some very stressful situations as a result. It was easier to put someone like Bill in the midst of turmoil and tension than deal with the person, often the pastor, who was responsible for creating the mess.

He needed a change of pace and routine. He began to consider the possibility, even wrote for information about sabbatical programs. I felt hopeful that he might move in that direction, as did the others. I was very pleased when he told me he refused the request to change to the other parish and assured me he would explore the possibility of taking a sabbatical in the next semester. A few days later, the new Archbishop called and asked him to meet with him the next day. When they met, the Archbishop told him he wanted him to take the pastorate in Bluff Lakes. The priests on the Personnel Board told him that Bill was self-effacing and needed some encouragement, but they thought he was perfect for that parish. From what Bill told me afterwards, he did try to tell the Archbishop about his fatigue and disillusionment and his desire for some time away. He called when he returned and told me the outcome.

"Marsha, I'll be leaving St. Hiltrudis to go to Bluff Lakes. The Archbishop told me the Personnel Board persuaded him to encourage me to do it."

"Bill, how could he even ask that of you? He doesn't know you, has no idea of how you've been struggling or of your need for time away. Did you tell him any of that?"

"Not really. I tried, but I just can't say 'No' to the Archbishop."

Bill was expected to report to the new parish within the next two weeks. That meant he would leave St. Hiltrudis without a pastor until the Personnel Board could begin the process of finding a replacement for him. The pastor at Bluff Lakes was leaving at the end of the week and it was critical that the new pastor be on board there as soon as possible.

The transition was unusually disruptive. Normally the out-going pastor would have the opportunity to assist in the orientation of his successor and have adequate time to bring closure to the years he served in the parish he was leaving. Bill had been there for more than ten years, and he was beloved by many of the parishioners. A very stressful time lay ahead for him and for them. We both suspected priority of placement was given to the affluent White parish.

I didn't want to overload Bill with my anger and distress, but I did need to pursue my feelings with the same friends who had been involved in encouraging him to take a sabbatical. When I told them what happened, Liz rolled her eyes and shrugged her shoulders. "That's the way the system works for the priests. God, when will the institution learn?"

Sharon, more traditional in some ways, added, "I'm sure the Spirit will take care of him. He will be good for those people. He is such a healer."

Nora was less resigned to that outcome. "I'm very concerned about him. That is not an easy parish. I taught there years ago, and it was very difficult. When people have money they are in the habit of believing they can influence life in all its dimensions, even in the Church. I really wish they hadn't done this."

"I feel like you, Nora, and I need to take some action. Bill is so compliant and passive at times that he makes me crazy. I was so sure he would take a sabbatical, but that's over now. The Archbishop hasn't even been here a month. Why did he even get involved?"

Bill seemed relieved that he did not have to tell his parishioners that his leaving was his own choice. He happily told them he had been asked to take the assignment and felt unable to deny the request. When he announced his change at Masses the next Sunday, there were outcries from those most involved in the parish life of St. Hiltrudis.

"How can they do this to us?"

"You've been so good for this parish."

"Why don't they leave us alone?"

"What gives them the right to think they can leave us without a pastor? Let the other parish do without in the interim."

"It's only because we're Black that they can do this. We're not as important as the wealthy Whites."

The mumblings echoed throughout the parish the next couple of weeks. This truly was a devastating thing to do to all the people involved. I knew I could not sit quietly, even though I was experienced enough with the political process of the Church to realize it was an act of futility. However, I needed to register my disapproval. Before I sent my letter, I cleared it with Bill and received his permission.

Dear Archbishop Benjamin:

I am writing to ask you to reconsider your appointment of Father William Creed as Pastor of Bluff Lakes. I feel you were perhaps unduly persuaded by the Personnel Board since you are so new to the archdiocese.

Bill has been active in parish ministry for more than thirty years; he has never taken time for his own personal renewal. Several of us close to him have been concerned lately; he is exhausted, disheartened, and desperately in need of some time away. To assign him to Bluff Lakes will create unbelievable tension for him.

Bill said he tried to talk with you about some of that, but he has a difficult time saying NO to his Archbishop. Please take some time to discuss this further with Bill and the Personnel Board and reconsider this assignment.

Sincerely in Christ,

Sister Marsha Malone

While I waited for a response, Bill commuted between the two parishes, a distance that required an hour and a half of travel each way. It was very strenuous for him and added to the fatigue and frustration he had begun to experience in dealing with the institution. I was not sure Archbishop Benjamin would respond, but he had announced upon his arrival in Chicago he would acknowledge every letter he received.

Since I lived about half-way between both parishes he was trying to serve, Bill and I arranged to meet one evening for dinner and a movie, for diversion as much as for enjoyment. I returned home about nine-thirty p.m. Bill departed for the south side parish almost immediately. He seemed very fatigued. I asked him to call when he arrived so I would know he was safe.

When I reached the door of my third-floor apartment, the phone was ringing. I rushed to the living room to answer it.

"Hello."

"Sister Marsha Malone, please," the familiar voice on the other end said. It was familiar because he had been on news and talk shows almost non-stop from the time of his arrival. I knew that voice.

"This is Marsha."

"This is Archbishop Benjamin. I received your letter and have been trying to write a response but I just couldn't seem to put into words what I wanted to say. I thought it best just to call and talk with you."

He acknowledged he was new and was trying to settle in.

"I guess I did take the Personnel Board's recommendation and their comments about Father Creed needing some encouragement very seriously. I am sorry if I made a mistake. I will do all I can to support him when he does relocate to Bluff Lakes."

"Archbishop Benjamin, I have been a friend of Bill's for many years and am aware of how much he needs some time and space away. The Parish to which you are sending him is a very difficult one to pastor. Bill is a wonderful priest and compassionate leader, but he will be thrust into a hornet's nest. Are you aware of the dynamics in that parish?"

"No, I only know what the Board told me."

"I can't help but feel that the system has superseded the value of the person in this situation. No one on the Personnel Board has contacted Bill for years; they have no idea where his life has taken him."

"I'm sorry, but I will do all I can to support him."

We concluded with promises of prayers for each other, and

he assured me he would remember Bill in his Masses. Nothing would change, but I had once again raised a question about the unchallenged method the institution used in dealing with people.

Bill called when he arrived home and listened quietly as I told him of the phone conversation. He sounded disappointed, I thought, and very tired. We didn't talk very long. I knew he needed to get some sleep.

Eventually, things settled down. A pastor was assigned to St. Hiltrudis and the daily commutes between both places came to an end for Bill. He could now settle in and begin to function in the new parish. Early on, he became aware that he had been thrust into a hot bed of factions and divisiveness. Within the first couple of weeks, he received a barrage of invitations to dinner from a variety of groups, all of them anxious to get his ear and support for their special projects and interests. He politely refused all the invitations. He knew as a result of reading the synopsis prepared by the Personnel Board that there were camps in the parish and each group was suspicious of the other.

Bill told me he felt it was best if he bought some time to sort through what was clearly a troublesome situation. I urged him to share that with the parish which he did in the bulletin. He asked for time to get his feet on the ground. He wanted to become more familiar with the parish so that he might serve it better, but he needed to do it his way. That received mixed reviews from some of the groups, but he had made the decision and would be guided by it. He did not like conflict and thrived in peaceful and cooperative situations.

CHAPTER TWENTY-TWO

Bill became aware of how challenging his role was. He was totally unsure he was effective. He did not share all the specifics of how he coped in the day-to-day. I knew he was experiencing a lot of tension, but I was shocked one afternoon to receive a call from him while I was at my office.

"Marsha, I'm in the hospital. I was having chest pains and drove to the doctor's, and he sent me directly here. I have Rosie in the car. Do you think you can come out here and pick her up?"

My heart almost stopped beating and my breath caught in my throat. "My God, Bill. Where are you? What room are you in?" I was frantic. If he died, I would really blast the system.

When I arrived at the hospital after a mildly hazardous drive, I went immediately to the emergency room. I was apprehensive and totally weak when I found him, lying on a gurney and punctured with multiple tubes. He looked so pale, but he smiled as I approached.

"Hey, kid, how are you?" That expression was one he used when he was frightened or uneasy. I knew this situation bothered him.

"Bill, I'm terrible, but I suspect I am much better than you. Tell me what happened."

He explained that he felt wretched all day and in the early afternoon drove to the doctor. From there, he explained how he landed in the emergency room. I was filled with concern and lots of questions, but Bill suggested we talk a little later. He reminded me that Rosie, his dog, was in the car and had been there for several hours. It was quite cold, but I knew she could wait a while longer. I wanted some assurance that Bill was stable before I left to care for the dog.

The nurse assured me he was in stable condition and Bill was clearly anxious about Rosie, so I went to the parking lot with his keys and located his car. When I reached it, Rosie was wagging her tail, happy to see me. I walked her a bit and then brought her to my car, which was still warm from the drive. She could wait there while I went back for another look at Bill. He was resting comfortably, the nurse told me, and assured me he was not in imminent danger. She told me to go home, and she'd call if anything changed. I hated to leave but Bill urged me to go and told me he'd call as soon as he was assigned to a room.

With heavy heart and sagging spirit, I trudged to the car. Rosie saw me coming and shifted from the driver's seat to the passenger seat. She loved to ride in the front seat. She was such a sensitive dog and realized I am sure, that something was amiss. I was a bit teary as I put the key in the ignition, and she laid her nose on my lap and raised her eyes to look at me. I reached over and petted her before we set off for home. When Bill called later that evening, he told me the emergency room doctor was pretty sure it was not his heart, but she wanted to keep him for several days for tests and observation. That made great sense to me and I urged him to rest. I'd call him in the morning and visit again after work the next day.

The diagnosis was stress and he was urged to slow down to avoid another episode. The experience frightened him, and we talked at length about what he could do to offset any further stress-related episodes. When he returned to the parish, he shared the incident with the parishioners and asked them to give him some time to develop his own style. Many of them complimented his style of celebrating liturgy and recognized his own deep spirituality. They wanted a pastor with those qualities rather than one who was a very efficient administrator. For the next several months, things seemed to continue on a more peaceful course for him.

In the meantime, I continued with my ministry, recruiting adult persons to live with physically and mentally challenged teens and adults in houses that created more home-like environments. With the advances in knowledge and medical care, youngsters who had Downs' Syndrome lived beyond their earlier life expectancy. They grew into adolescents and adults. This project involved the creation of a neighborhood community in which nine of these homes would eventually be located.

It was a wonderful experience to come into contact with persons willing to commit to life in this type of home for a limited period of time. One of my tasks was to create opportunities for them to develop and deepen their own spirituality, a critical necessity if they were to continue to function effectively. Coming to know the mentally challenged teens and adults was also very enriching. It was a joy and delight to witness their spontaneous joy and enthusiasm. I was also the person who was to facilitate problems that might occur.

It was a peaceful experience for the most part, although inevitable tensions and crises arose as might be expected. I knew I would only be there until I could get this community established and then would move on. The role would become much more administrative once things were in place and would require that I become licensed in a field in which I was not interested. I had great respect for those involved in health care, but it was not something that attracted me. My training and experience was along another track, so to speak.

Bill made plans for the parish and knew of my expertise and interest in adult formation. While his staff in Bluff Lakes was larger than he had in St. Hiltrudis, there was no one who was trained to minister in that capacity. So, in addition to my work with the community building project, I began a leadership training program in his parish on a once a month basis. It was a wonderful experience for me and for those who participated. They would then become more active in ministering to the needs of the parish. However, as the structure became more complex, Bill felt less adequate. Administration was not his strength and the growing involvement and activity of the members of the parish required coordination and facilitation.

So it was that I accepted the position of Pastoral Associate there. It was quite different from the experience in St. Hiltrudis. Some strong right-wing people in the parish in Bluff Lakes remained determined to have nothing change, even though some very interested and involved persons wanted to explore new ways of being a parish and were open to changes in many ways. Those who wanted to hold fast to the rules and regulations vocally criticized any variations. The others relished the opportunities to experience greater participation and involvement.

My role was to continue to form and develop persons to assume leadership roles and to do the formal training of ministers of care and communion, lectors and facilitators of the Christ Renews His Parish retreats that we began. Things moved well and smoothly for the most part, but there was always the undercurrent from those opposed to the changes. The parish thrived; there was renewed life and spirit. More and more people began to praise Bill for his leadership and spirituality.

The other staff members excelled in their own areas of responsibility, and we generated new programs and activities. Of course, some secretly criticized and questioned Bill's and my obvious friendship. By now, though, we moved to another level for the most part and our physical intimacy was much less troublesome to us. Lapses occurred from time to time, but we managed to handle them more easily and returned to balance and commitment.

I was becoming more alert and sensitive to the exclusion of women in many dimensions of Church and that was beginning to impact my ministry. My understanding of feminist was someone who valued the contributions of both male and female, but felt the latter were underrepresented in church and liturgical functions. I became an intimate part of the pastoral team in the parish and wanted a more public role in worship opportunities. This led to a new crisis.

CHAPTER TWENTY THREE

This awareness of feminism evolved over several years, the result of my experiences, reading and graduate studies. I no longer felt included in church liturgy. The Scriptures told of stories written for men or brothers. I could no longer relate to an exclusively male God who was Father, Master or Lord. I yearned to hear the Word of God proclaimed by females as well as males. I longed to hear homilies that spoke to my experience as a woman. I knew I was not alone in this. My conversations with a growing number of women revealed their pain at being excluded in public liturgical events also.

It became a source of such unrest for me that I knew I needed to try to do something that would offer a more inclusive presentation of the feminine in worship, at least where I ministered. The pastoral staff had already introduced girl servers, even though the Archbishop and the Pope announced that was not to be. There were women lectors and ministers of communion. It was not enough.

Bill understood my frustration and disappointment at the limitations placed on my preaching because I was a woman. It pained him to see me so angry and upset. He was frustrated and felt powerless to do anything until the rules changed. He appreciated my gifts and knew how well they were received at St. Hiltrudis. He wanted more of the parishioners in Bluff Lakes to experience them as well. He fully supported an increased role for women, including ordination.

We did some research and found some legitimate opportunities available to me to give occasional homilies. After contact with a specialist in Canon Law, we began slowly to include me on the schedule of homilists. Given the strong right-wing population, we knew we could expect some flack, but we refused to allow them to have free reign in shaping the life of the parish.

I was extremely nervous the first time I gave the homily. The liturgy was a commissioning of the ministers I trained for outreach to the sick and homebound. In the norms, this was an occasion on which someone with primary responsibility for the group could preach. It was a powerful experience to break open the Word of God, connect it to daily life from my perspective as a woman, and open new reflections for those who listened with open hearts and minds. I could tell, as my gaze swept the congregation, that many were open, but the scowling faces of others gave their clear message. I looked away from them so as not to distract myself from the words I spoke.

After Mass, many approached Bill and I and applauded this change. They praised Bill for his courage and initiative. Others, though, rallied the 'conservatives' and wrote to Bill. They accused us of flagrant disobedience and "flying in the face of the Holy Father." They lamented the fact that *Sister Marsha didn't know her place*. Bill's attempt to inform the parish of the process we used in allowing this change fell on deaf ears. When they failed to dissuade Bill from this course, they undertook a letter-writing campaign to have me removed from the pulpit, and perhaps even from ministry.

So it was that Bill received a letter from the Bishop of our region. Harry wrote that there were complaints about my preaching, and he wanted to talk with him about that. There was no problem with the content of the homily but with the gender of the homilist. Bill withheld the letter for several days, reluctant to open the pain and hurt and diminishment I felt on those occasions.

When he finally brought it to the staff meeting, there was no response. They were unwilling to open the possibility for changes, and they generally did not support greater inclusivity for women in the Mass, until and unless the Pope spoke. I was not surprised at their unwillingness to take a position in this regard. This was routine for that group. I was very upset, though, that the Bishop had not even considered that I should be included in the conversation. This could impact my ministry and perhaps even my lifestyle, and I was determined to have some input.

When the staff meeting ended, I left the room immediately, although the entire group dispersed without much conversation, reluctant to have any discussion, even informally, about this issue. I went to my office, tried to quiet myself and determined what kind of action I would take. I reached for the phone and dialed the Bishop's office. He and I had known each other for several years, even before he was named a bishop, in fact, and we were on a first-name basis.

"Bishop Mrozynski speaking." I was totally surprised that he was the one who answered.

"Harry, this is Marsha Malone. Bill Creed just brought to the staff meeting the letter he received from you about my preaching."

"I'm glad he did. I've been waiting for a call from him to discuss it."

"I can't believe you and he plan to discuss my ministry without my being present."

"I'm Bill's bishop, Marsha, and I need to talk with him first."

"Aren't you my bishop as well, Harry?" I could feel my pressure rising and I heard the edge in his voice.

"Yes, of course, but I need to respect the hierarchy involved. Bill is pastor and priest. I planned to talk with you after I met with him. Surely you know from your own leadership experience the need to respect the chain of command."

"That, Harry, is one of the key problems in the church today. Masculine and feminine models of leadership are very different. Women in religious communities come from a perspective of inclusivity not hierarchy. All persons involved in a decision are included in the conversation. Hierarchy does not respect persons."

His response was weak, something mumbled about differences in opinion but his need to follow his own set of principles. We bid farewell somewhat less graciously than we would have under different circumstances. I knew there was no resolution, but for the moment, I consoled myself with the knowledge that I had expressed myself directly to him.

Bill left the office after the staff meeting to visit the hospital. That was often a place he retreated to when there was tension. He found comfort and solace with the sick and dying, and it helped him to put his own suffering in perspective. When he returned and went to his office, I told him about my phone call. His usual ruddy color drained. He became quite agitated and started to rearrange the piles on his desk. He did not like confrontation. Within a few minutes, the phone rang and the secretary said Bishop Mrozynski was on the line.

I couldn't hear what he said, but clearly it was a push to have the meeting. When they agreed on a date, I heard Bill ask, "What about Marsha?"

I didn't hear the reply, but it was brief. I waited with apprehension as Bill completed his conversation with Harry.

"What did he say about me?"

"Bring her."

The next few days were overshadowed with the uncertainty of the outcome of our pending conversation. Bill and I reviewed the process that led to our decision to allow me to preach. I knew he was very nervous, not so much for the fact that he might be chastised, but because he was fearful of what might happen to me.

When we met in the parking lot of the Bishop's residence that Saturday morning, I was struck by the fact that Bill's body reflected the heaviness I presumed he felt. He seemed stooped, as though carrying a very heavy load. I knew I looked tired after a restless night, but he looked far worse I thought. Neither of us knew what to expect from the meeting, but we suspected the outcome could have significant consequences for both of us.

"Bill you look so pale. Are you feeling okay?"

"Not really. I think I have a touch of the flu. I'll be okay. How are you?"

"Nervous and scared. I'll be glad when this is over."

We moved to the doorway with some speed, anxious to get this meeting over with. Surprisingly, although it was Saturday, the secretary was on duty, and she led us from the entrance to a small parlor. When Harry joined us, the room became significantly smaller. He was not a large man, but he symbolized the authority of the institutional Church at that moment and that seemed quite big at this point. He smiled, greeted us cordially and we all shook hands. He realized, I was quite sure, how tense each of us was. It seemed obvious to me that he would have preferred being anywhere else in any other kind of conversation than this one.

"You're both doing such good work at that parish. I have received letters from people about how enriched they feel the parish has been by both of your ministries."

Apparently those who supported what we did were finally beginning to let their voices be heard. We had strategized about that and encouraged our supporters to write letters to that effect. Good for them and for us. Unfortunately, the common practice in the Church is only to squeak when something pinches but to remain silent when everything is going well. In this day and age, it was necessary for the satisfied parishioners to speak because those who resisted change had pen and paper in hand at the first sign of a variation.

Bill thanked him for his words of affirmation and began, "Harry, I'd like to let you know how and why we reached the decision to allow Marsha to preach. She does it very rarely. In fact I wish she could speak more often. She's very good and reaches many people. I'm not even sure how many are opposed to her preaching, but they always seem to get the attention. We checked with John Logger, the Canonist, and he assured us we were within the outside limits of the law."

"It's been wonderful for me, Harry. The only time I preach is when it involves the groups I have been working with. Since I really get to know them well in the course of their training, it seems to follow that I play a part in their commissioning or their reception into the Church, in the case of the Rite of Christian Initiation of Adults. I want to preach more often. It is very moving for me to reflect on and share the impact of Scripture on life."

Harry sat quietly, his blue eyes moving from one of us to the other as we spoke. When he responded, it was not a replay of the norms and rules regarding women in liturgy, but a grateful appreciation for all we were doing to promote deeper spirituality in the parish.

"I read your parish bulletin every week, and I'm impressed with the kinds of programs you are offering and the groups you are developing. You're really focusing on spirituality, which is so very necessary today. You're both very effective ministers and are doing a great job in the parish."

I did not expect that affirmation. I hoped it wasn't the prelude to a refusal to allow me to continue to preach. It seemed to me there was softness in Harry that wasn't there when I spoke with him several days earlier. I was very glad I had pushed for my inclusion in this meeting; perhaps it would shape a different outcome. Harry wasn't an enemy, but he was trapped by his own position in the hierarchy. He reminded us of what a difficult time this was in the Church. There was a need to incorporate new ways into old structures and it was a tight fit. He agreed that we operated within a legitimate, albeit fluid, boundary of Canon Law.

"Marsha, I'm quite sure you are a good homilist. I might even want to hear you myself."

Bill added, "She is well prepared and gives an excellent homily."

When we left, we took with us Harry's tacit but guarded approval to continue as we had been doing. The resolution was hazy, fuzzy and specific to this situation. There was no public statement from the Bishop about our meeting and apparently he wrote no response to the people who sent the original letter to him. As a result, within a short time, the people determined to preserve the status quo just went to higher authorities.

CHAPTER TWENTY-FOUR

Bill and I spent a few minutes in the parking lot. His color returned, I thought. We both realized we bought a tenuous permission. It was unlikely that Harry would publicly communicate the outcome, and we would once again be left with having to cope with the discrepancy between the public and private pronouncements of the hierarchy. Harry supported women's ordination, I knew, but he would never state that publicly either. How will anything ever change in such a structure?

We continued on our path and for the moment received no letters condemning our actions. I knew that didn't mean people had changed, but they were probably continuing to pursue another level of authority. They might even go to Rome. They would be heard there.

When it was time to renew my contract, I announced my resignation. Bill and I talked about it at length. I was very weary; being an advocate for women in the Church was draining my enthusiasm and depleting my energy and enthusiasm. The pursuit of the right wing took a significant toll.

I was ready for a new ministry, although I had no clear sense of what that might be. I knew it was not within the institutional Church, I was depleted from the almost daily struggles with the system. My skills, orientation and training became more focused on feminist theology and spirituality, and I wanted to pursue that.

During the course of the last two years I was at the parish, I participated in the Doctor of Ministry program, a creative formation and education package developed by one of the innovative faculty members at the major seminary. He designed the program to allow women to receive higher education in a seminary setting. Heretofore, women were not allowed to take part in the theological and ministerial programs at the seminary, nor were we permitted to enter the classes with the men who were preparing for priesthood so our courses took place off-campus.

It was an invigorating and visionary experience for me. The central theme of the two years was learning the art of theological reflection, a method of accessing the movement and action of the Spirit at the center of our own lives. It was not based on hierarchy nor on orthodoxy and was, therefore, very refreshing. The participants included religious women, priests, as well as men and women not in religious life or priesthood. We met one day a week and three times a year for a three-day intensive, which was held on the seminary campus.

In order to complete the requirements for the Degree of Doctor of Ministry, I would have to design a project in which I trained persons to learn the art of theological reflection and use it to make decisions about the presence of God in their lives. I had not yet identified the specific project, but I fully expected it would engage me in ministry with women searching for more in their own lives and for prayer forms that would speak to them more personally.

When Bill received a call from the Cardinal just two weeks before I planned to leave parish ministry, I knew my decision was timely and absolutely necessary. The Cardinal, elevated from Archbishop, was the same person who had promised to support Bill after he assigned him to Bluff Lakes. The Cardinal told him he held a letter from the Vatican Office stating quite clearly that Sister Marsha Malone was no longer to preach. Bill told the Cardinal how disappointed he was with the process and how discouraged he was with that segment of the parish so opposed to change and the incredible power they seemed to wield with Rome. This latest incident only sharpened his realization of how influential with the institutional Church his opponents were.

"It's too late. She will be leaving parish ministry in two weeks. Her decision will leave a gaping hole in this parish as a result. In the long run, the Church has lost a gifted and visionary woman. It's very unfortunate that we are forcing such people to seek other avenues to share their gifts. I'm also very uncomfortable with the influence the conservatives have with you and with Rome." He sounded much bolder than before. In truth, these struggles had taken their toll on him, too. I don't know if the Cardinal heard in Bill's voice his own growing disenchantment with parish and institutional Church ministry.

Apparently, there was another casualty in this conflict. Bishop Mrozynski was transferred to a diocese in which most of the parishes were in the wilderness. The parishes under his jurisdiction had a farewell celebration for him. I had an opportunity to chat with him on that occasion.

"Harry, I am sorry for this change. I know it removes you from family and friends and familiar places. I want to thank you again for your openness to dialogue and your willingness to expand your view. I wish you the best in your new assignment."

"Marsha, I was a fairly conservative priest when I was first made a Bishop, but contacts with people like you have formed me into a more liberal leader. I honestly wonder whether this new assignment is advancement or banishment to the wilderness."

"You may never know for sure, Harry. However, it sounds to me like you will have more freedom to initiate some creative changes. That's the diocese with several parishes whose pastors are women and non-ordained ministers, isn't it?"

"Yes, and I was told the people are very open and receptive to innovation. They are just grateful to have functioning parishes in their regions." Harry smiled easily.

"If it weren't so far from home, I might consider applying for one of those positions as pastor. You'd love to have me there, wouldn't you?" We both chuckled at that prospect.

The parish had a wonderful farewell celebration for me, allowing me to savor the good and enlivening experiences I had there. I knew I was different in many ways than when I started. The eagerness and enthusiasm of many to explore new horizons in spirituality and prayer forms challenged me to further study and personal growth as well. I said good-bye at all the Masses the Sunday before I terminated there, although I was not able to give the homily. I would preach one more time in that church, but had no idea of the day, hour or circumstances.

CHAPTER TWENTY-FIVE

I began to develop the Doctor of Ministry Project as soon as I left the parish. I had no idea how I would ever use that degree as I didn't see myself returning to institutional Church ministry, but it seemed important for me to bring the studies to completion. It might be a helpful credential in the future. I organized a series of meetings over the course of a year in which ten women who agreed to participate in the process would gather once a month for input, reflection and discussion on the role and relationship of women to the institutional church.

It was an energizing project, one that encouraged the women to share their own experiences and then draw the conclusions they could from it in light of the role of women in the Church. I missed the opportunity to share in planning as I had with Bill in the parish, but the lonely work paid off when we met as a group. This was developing into a really exciting experience, one that eventually resulted in the development of a new ministerial site.

The Berakah Community developed out of this project. It was located in an old three-story building that had recently been a boarding house, although it was owned by a community of religious sisters anxious to have it rented for another purpose. When I saw the place, I felt it was perfect for what I was trying to do, and the Province was willing to assist with rent and the funding for me and another sister I invited to join in this endeavor. I wanted to have a companion and also realized the Province might be more receptive if I involved someone from our religious community.

When the other sister joined the group, she appeared in tune with the direction I was taking but in time I realized she and I were not on the same wave length. I designed and implemented the project to complete my degree and shared the essentials with her. This was a new beginning for me, and I eagerly looked forward to the development of this center. I was sensitive to the fact that I needed to make some compromises, but I was not willing to succumb to her discomfort with "feminist spirituality." This was precisely at the heart of my project and non negotiable. This fundamental difference in orientation and goals soon led to the diminishment of the eagerness and hope with which I began the project. We worked together in some ways initially, and I thrived briefly in that situation.

Leaving the parish had been a good thing for me, even though it meant seeing less of Bill, but we were in almost daily phone contact. His voice so often reflected his fatigue and discouragement and loneliness in ministry. We saw each other at least once a week. Very shortly I became aware that he was becoming more haggard looking, slouched and depressed. Perhaps that was not entirely new, but the added distance gave me a new perspective on him. I became concerned and urged him to make an appointment for a physical, which might identify any health issues that contributed to his diminished energy.

I was aware of some of the difficulties with his staff, some of whom used him when it would benefit their special projects or interests, but who carefully distanced from him when he was attacked by the "power-elite" on whom they relied for financial and personal support.

"Marsha, I know you're happier away from here. I can see the change in you. I miss your presence and contribution to the staff meetings. I never seem to know how to say what I mean or to respond to some of the reservations and nay saying at the meetings. You were always much better at that than I. I don't really feel there is much support for what I propose either. I am the pastor, but I feel powerless to accomplish what I would like to see happen in the parish."

"I may have been more vocal and articulate, Bill, but I seldom felt good about most of my interactions with them. It seemed like the only time we could function effectively was when we had a facilitator or consultant present. On those occasions, we seemed better able to move forward, but the difficulties in communication returned as soon as we tried to implement any new directions."

"I don't feel like I can trust some of them. Occasionally, I've heard from parishioners that this or that comment or criticism was made by a member of the staff. At times, I feel they are trying to discredit me."

"I'm not surprised. You know how I feel about a couple of them. They are not really team players, except when it is to their benefit. Even at this distance from daily involvement I hear comments that suggest there is a growing divisiveness among some of the groups in the parish. It's as though there are 'your people, her people' and 'his people.' Maybe it's finally time for you to take the sabbatical you missed when you began this pastorate."

He shared with me his conversation with Ernie, one of his most loyal supporters in the beginning of his ministry there. Ernie became embroiled in the controversy that arose about the non-renewal of a contract of a staff member. That person fueled the conflict by sharing her distorted version of the story. She had the ear of some influential people in the parish, and they began to discredit his ability to function effectively as an administrator. To Bill's surprise, he learned that Ernie was spearheading the group.

He approached him and arranged to meet with him so that he might share his perspective on the matter. Bill and Ernie met for lunch at a local restaurant. Ernie began, "Bill, I'm aware from my background in business administration that there are always at least two sides to every story. I'd be happy to hear yours."

Bill shared as much as he could without betraying any confidential information, but there was nothing he said that persuaded Ernie to reconsider his questioning of the non-renewal of Marilyn's contract.

As he recounted the conversation to me later, he sounded even more disheartened. "Ernie seemed interested in what I had to say, but he was clearly more sympathetic to Marilyn. She spent many hours with them over the last few weeks. Her tears and accusations of being treated unfairly fell on receptive ears. I honestly don't know how she could have said what she did."

He said the conversation ended when he told Ernie, "It's really not fun any more. I used to love being in a parish, but I'm losing my zest."

Recently retired from his company, Ernie told Bill he knew what that felt like and that was one of the reasons he made the decision to leave. He added in a tone that triggered an uncomfortable emotional reaction in Bill, "Maybe it's time for you to think about that, too."

Bill was flattered by that suggestion and felt betrayed by Ernie. However, it nurtured the growth of the seed I planted some weeks earlier, one which quickly matured as the undermining accelerated. I never understood the reasons for the active and subversive aggression of some of the staff. I did know Bill was a more effective pastor than administrator. He was a compassionate and deeply spiritual leader who was out of his realm as the parish became more complex and highly organized and politicized. He was a trusting person who could not imagine people would in any way be deliberately malicious. But they were.

Gradually he became aware of the change in himself. When we spent time together, he was tired and almost seemed listless. Clearly the passion had gone out of his ministry. I recognized some of the symptoms from my own past experiences. We talked about it one day as we walked along the shore of the lake.

"You know, Marsha, I've been thinking a lot about my conversation with Ernie Jackson a couple of months ago. I was initially hurt and put off by his suggestion that it might be time for me to go. Lately, however, I've begun to think he might be right. What do you think?"

You know how I feel. I suggested you make that change several months ago. I know what I've been seeing and hearing from you for a while now, and it's not life or energy or enthusiasm. I've been worried that your health may be deteriorating. Have you given any more thought to having that physical I suggested a while back? Nothing is worth losing your health over. You're still too young to succumb to that."

"My last doctor's appointment was last summer for the prostate exam. That was fine. I don't think I'm sick, just tired. I think I'm just too tired." He sounded every bit of that. Unfortunately, it was more than tiredness, but that didn't become apparent immediately.

CHAPTER TWENTY-SIX

Within a short time, Bill began to plan for a sabbatical. He contacted the Cardinal to explain why he wished to terminate as pastor and expressed his need and desire for time away. The Cardinal was very responsive to his request and even apologized for the difficult situation he placed him in when he assigned him to that parish. He told Bill he would ask a member of the committee on sabbaticals to contact him and give him all the assistance he needed. He would have a year off for this renewal time. The Cardinal told Bill he expected him to return to a parish at the end of that time.

Bill solicited information from many sources on possible renewal experiences and eventually devised a program that would allow him to have extended personal time at his home in Elk Lake as well as more structured time. Some of that time included a renewal program for priests in California. That would last for three months in the fall. He would then return home around Thanksgiving time and remain there until he began the second program, a retreat/workshop in Centering Prayer in Colorado. He became quite excited about what was ahead.

The parish held a wonderful farewell party for him. Many expressed their deep regret that he would not be returning to that parish after his time away. There was a sense of loss and grief among the majority of parishioners, it seemed. However, they began to see a new light-heartedness returning to Bill and they rejoiced in that for him. Those who cared for him became quite concerned at his diminishing enthusiasm and energy.

He delighted in the time to do some repairs and remodeling on his home in Wisconsin and seemed to welcome the quiet time. I continued to spend my one day a week off with him and contributed in whatever way I could. I was pleased with what I saw as the weeks went on. I knew this kind of time would be very rewarding. I was happy he had it; although I dreaded the day he would leave for three months in California. When I took him to the airport, I felt a significant pit develop in my stomach, anticipating the loneliness I would experience.

We kept in close touch during that time, although our phone calls and correspondence confirmed that each of us was on a different path toward the future. Bill was surrounded by priests, the only participants in this program. While he found a growing dissonance between what many of them valued, he still insisted he needed to remain a priest.

He was not surprised, however, when I shared the developments in my own life. The conflict of which he was very aware at the Berakah Community eventually led to the dissolution of the Center. That added fuel to the engine that was driving me to complete the Doctor of Ministry Degree. I set aside significant time to write the details of the project for submission to the Board of Regents. There was a growing urgency to bring this to completion, to finalize the degree and bring closure to those years of my life. It was in the writing of this that I confirmed my conviction that I could no longer remain in religious life—the very underpinnings that held me for many years no longer sustained me.

Bill preferred that I not make any changes. He feared I would lose credibility and become less effective in ministry. I knew I needed to make this move to have credibility with myself. It was not only church and the devaluation of women; it was our relationship as well. I was increasingly less able to live with the struggle to integrate that into my present commitment, and I was not at peace with myself.

I alternated between marvel and anger at his ability to compartmentalize our relationship, admittedly the most significant relationship in his life. I learned, though, that males are much more able to do this than females. That masculine trait has probably contributed to the present crisis in the Catholic Church; priests segment their personal lives from their public ministerial lives and bishops distance their personal convictions from the orthodoxy espoused by Rome.

After a series of meetings with the Provincial, she concurred with my decision to begin the process of dispensation, one that could take many weeks. My first step was to draft a letter to her requesting the release from my vows and stating the reason. I wrote that I no longer found the structures of religious and ecclesial life capable of sustaining my spirit. When Linda received my letter, she called and advised me that my reason would not be acceptable to Rome and would only delay the process. I needed to state that I was no longer able to live the vowed life. Once more I experienced the diminishment of person at the hands of the structure. So be it! I needed freed of the conflicts and constraints.

When Bill returned from his second renewal experience, he was delighted to see me looking so happy and peaceful. The sense of freedom and new life I experienced flooded my spirit and persuaded him that I had indeed made the right choice. In his absence I completed the draft of the Doctor of Ministry Book. Two readers assigned by the seminary were working on it, and I was waiting for their comments and suggested revisions. I was pleased with the research I had done to support my thesis that the institutional Church was sexist. The theological reflection of the core group over the course of the year further supported the fact that many women experienced the same kind of sexism. Bill began to look at his options for the future as well, but not as radically as I. He knew he was burnt out on institutional ministry and needed to be about something else that was more life-giving. He was becoming more open to creative alternatives to nurture his evolving spirituality.

The Centering Prayer retreat and workshop touched him deeply, and he really wanted to try to promote its practice among groups of people. Parish was too demanding in terms of administration for him to consider that as a focal setting.

CHAPTER TWENTY-SEVEN

S o it was that we began to explore the creation of some sort of spirituality center in which each of us could share our gifts and nurture our passions for ministry. It never occurred to me that I would not continue in some sort of ministry, although it would not be within the institutional church. Bill was more caught since he was a priest, but he hoped to persuade the Cardinal that he needed something other than parish for his next assignment. With that in mind, we looked around the area for possible sites in which to begin this new development. If necessary, he would return to parish work part-time, but he would seek permission to develop Centering Prayer workshops and retreats.

The retreat he made during the sabbatical and the subsequent workshops moved him deeply. He was drawn by the image of a God who was at the center of who he was, a God who calls to life and wholeness. In those experiences he discovered a God whose will is less tied to institutional religion and more intimately linked to life at the deepest level of each and every person.

If we could find a suitable building, we could start to plan toward that center. I was hopeful because I needed a place to live as well as a means to earn an income. Ministry was all I knew. With all those options whirling in our heads, we entered the Real Estate Office in town to see an agent. While we waited, I looked at the pictures of houses that lined the walls of the foyer. My gaze was drawn to a barn structure and I called to Bill, "Look at this. It could be perfect—a place for our spirituality and centering prayer workshops and a home for me. What do you think?"

He smiled sheepishly as he often did when I made what appeared to be implausible statements. "I don't know, Marsha. Maybe we could look at it."

"Let's do that. It's probably not what it looks like but if we see it, and then we'll know it's outrageous and we can look further."

A few minutes later, Clarisse arrived and introduced herself. She was quite happy to take us to the facility. The exterior looked every bit like an old barn, but there were some wonderful accommodations. The door of the hayloft through which the original occupants received their meals was suspended below and that opening was now a picture window that overlooked the property. Beneath the old hay-loft door two sets of windows opened up to a kitchen. To the left of the main building was a greenhouse.

The outside was wonderful, and I could feel the excitement building as we entered the interior of the structure. A small mud room greeted us first, and then a heavy green door opened to the full barn. As we opened that door, I was totally delighted with what I saw. "Bill, look at those skylights! This barn wood is so neat. I've always loved wood. And look at the fire-place. It's huge!" It was located in the center of the main room, whose ceilings stretched to the stars. It was a marvelous red brick fireplace with a chimney suspended on large chains from the roof. I was twirling in all directions. This was such a wonderful place. Beyond the fireplace was a small whitewashed bedroom, whose walls were outlined with delightful stencils. It offered a marked but welcome contrast to the dark brown barn-wooded living room.

At the opposite end of the room there was a rustic dining table and benches. Beyond that was the greenhouse. I rushed over to open the sliding doors and stepped onto the tiled floor. I looked at Bill, aware that my enthusiasm might have been more than he was feeling at that point.

He turned to Clarisse with a sort of helpless look and said, "I knew when I saw the greenhouse that it was all over. Marsha is crazy about plants. I can just see her puttering in there."

As he spoke, I scurried past them and up the open staircase to the next floor, a loft space that accommodated two bedrooms and two baths and a floor-to ceiling set of book shelves. "Bill, come on up. Wait until you see this." When he reached the top of the stairs, I was no longer on the floor but climbing an old playground slide ladder, which led to the tiny loft. I moved to the window and saw the view for miles. I was already dreaming how this could be used for gatherings. Bill was usually a little slower in envisioning alternatives, so I started to plant the seeds immediately.

Clarisse looked as though she was thoroughly enjoying the interaction as well as suspecting she might have a sale. At that point, she thought we were a couple looking for a second home or perhaps a full-time residence.

"Would you like to see the outside?" she asked.

"Yes, of course," we responded in unison. By now, I could see Bill was sharing some of my enthusiasm for the possibilities this place offered. His eyes were much brighter, and his smiling countenance gave its own message. He was so charming when he smiled that way.

Even though we had driven down the long driveway from the road, neither of us had noticed the grounds. The first thing that caught our attention now was the structure of the barn itself. Then we looked out over the five-acre parcel and saw several clusters of large trees, cottonwood, we later learned. Most of the ground was covered with overgrown field grass. The trees needed pruning and the entire space needed grooming before it could serve our needs, but it held real potential, I thought.

Our spirituality had expanded in recent years to include creation and nature as essential components. This place could offer a respite for persons looking for opportunities for solitude and retreat as well as create a setting for groups to come together for the same kinds of experiences.

Clarisse interrupted our dreaming when she said, "Marsha, you never even saw the kitchen."

I laughed. "You're right, but that's not my stronghold."

Bill nodded his assent. We entered the house again and turned to the right beyond the green door. There was a compact L-shaped kitchen, which led to the small alcove that was the dining room.

We left there with reluctance. I was euphoric and I couldn't wait to talk with Bill without the presence of Clarisse to see if and how we might purchase this property. We thanked Clarisse for her time and explained a little of what we were thinking while remaining cautious and guarded in suggesting a follow-up. Was this the hand of God in our lives once again? It all seemed like an impossible dream. *Would I ever really live and minister here?*

CHAPTER TWENTY-EIGHT

One other piece of business remained for Bill to tend to during his sabbatical and that was to get his annual physical. Four years earlier, during a routine physical his doctor discovered an enlarged prostate. He was referred to a specialist for a biopsy, which turned out negative. Although there was no malignancy, it was a clear sign to him that he needed to keep a close check on things. His father had died of prostate cancer. Bill consulted annually with an urologist from that time on and received a clean bill of health. That was not true this year.

We were looking forward to what we could develop at the Barn property when he received a call from his doctor's office. Bill's last prostate exam showed some changes, and the doctor ordered an MRI. He wanted to see Bill about the results of the test. We were both very apprehensive when that test was ordered, although we didn't yet know the purpose of that was to determine whether and how far the cancer had spread into his spinal column. We didn't know either that the prostate was cancerous.

Bill was alone at his home in Elk City when he received the news. He called me at the Women's Center almost immediately.

I knew from his voice and the staccato-like replay of his conversation with the nurse that he was shocked and apprehensive.

"Marsha, I got a call from Doctor Jackson's nurse a few minutes ago. He wants to see me as soon as possible about the test results. I'm going into Bluff Lakes tomorrow at 9:00 a.m."

"I'll meet you there. I'm very concerned." My voice cracked and betrayed the tears that flooded my eyes. Suddenly the phone line carried the wracking sobs of both of us. I regretted that he was alone in Wisconsin at that moment. I wanted to be there with him to hold him and be held by him. This was terrifying news.

"No, Marsha, I hate to take your time. I'll meet you at my house later."

I couldn't see the point of waiting in Wisconsin while he was driving to the doctor's office, which was only ten minutes from my home. It would be a terribly anxious wait. I'd rather be in the reception area and be there when he finished with the appointment. I persisted in my request and that subdued his reluctance. We talked several times on the phone that day, each of us trying to shore the other up.

The next morning, we arrived at the doctor's office simultaneously. Our wordless hug communicated the depth of our emotions. We entered the empty waiting room, professional but sterile, lined with the usual display of insipid magazines characteristic of such places. The nurse-receptionist was not at her perch, so we sat in two of the chairs provided. Our silence echoed in the room as we groped for words to dispel the tension each of us felt.

"Did you sleep well last night, Bill?"

"Not really. How about you?"

"Not much at all. I'll be glad when this is over, and we're sure what we're dealing with."

At that moment the receptionist appeared and invited him to come into the inner office. We agreed the day before that I would wait for him in the reception area while he met with the doctor. However, as he moved to the door, he signaled me to come with him. I was reluctant, knowing this was a personal situation, and a sexual one at that. The doctor and others in the office attended Church at Bluff Lakes and knew both of us. They might feel uncomfortable if I went into the office with him. *To hell with them.* Bill wanted me with him, and that was all there was to it.

When we sat down in the doctor's office, I said, "Bill, I'll leave when the doctor arrives so you can be alone with him." I knew I was groping for some way to avoid the full impact of the diagnosis I expected.

"No, I want you to stay. I know you'll hear things I might miss. I want you to stay."

I felt awkward when the doctor arrived and looked at me with eyes that seemed to reflect his question about my presence. Not one to run from the difficult situation, I asked, "Do you have a problem with my being here?"

His handsome face was impassive above his tall frame, and he turned to Bill and said, "It's your call, Father."

"I want her to stay."

With that, he whipped out several X-rays and splattered them across the screen on his back wall. "I have good news and bad news. What do you want to hear first?"

Bill responded, "Let's hear the bad news."

"Your PSA count was very high, an indication of the presence of cancer. The normal route of prostate cancer is to move into the spine. That was the reason for the MRI. As you can see from these proofs, there are multiple tumors in your spinal column."

Even with our eyes riveted on the lighted wall behind his desk, we were unable to grasp what he was saying. The clarifications and information he shared did nothing to dispel the dread with which we had arrived in this place. We both slumped in our physician-office chairs. I didn't even want to look at Bill then for fear I would see his tears through my own wet eyes. The physician paused a moment as he looked from one of us to the other. Then he added, "Now for the good news."

Is there ever any good news when cancer enters the picture? We both had too many family members and friends who succumbed to this insidious disease.

Doctor Jackson proceeded, "There have been some recent developments in the treatment of prostate cancer, even when it has metastasized to the bone. Lupron appears to offer significant changes in the spread of prostate cancer. It's an injection that must be taken each month on the same date. If the type of cancer you have is hormone sensitive, it will destroy the cancer cells and restore the build-up of the bones that have been damaged by the disease."

This sounded a bit preposterous to me, but I was open to the possibility of a miracle.

The doctor continued, "It is relatively new, though, and the long-term effectiveness has not yet been determined. It may be that you will have to seek another treatment process in ten years. The way they are working on prostate cancer cures, there will no doubt be something else available if it becomes necessary to discontinue Lupron."

Well, that did sound like good news but that was a big if. Suppose the cancer was not hormone sensitive? There was no way to know that in advance, so we might as well begin the treatment program today. Bill received his first injection, and we left the office. Once outside, we entered our separate cars with little fanfare. We drove to Bill's home in Wisconsin. I followed his car all the way, anguished at the possibility that the day might come when this drive might be one I would have to make alone.

When we arrived at Bill's, neither of us possessed the will or the energy to do any further dreaming about the proposed future ministry. We just wanted to be together. We drove to the Barn just to keep our hopes alive, but for that day the dream seemed remote and improbable. However, in a few weeks, the deed was ours.

CHAPTER TWENTY-NINE

In those ensuing weeks, we vacillated between dread and apprehension, and optimism and exuberance. The dread was, of course, occasioned by Bill's cancer. He made contact with a physician in Elk Lakes who would see that he continued to receive the Lupron injection every month. He would monitor the PSA count as well. Chris offered Bill hope and encouraged him to pursue the development of the spirituality center; one he felt was sorely needed.

I received copies of the Doctor of Ministry draft from my readers, and there were surprisingly few revisions, none of them major. I made the suggested changes, resubmitted the copies to them and had been notified I would receive the Doctor of Ministry Degree at the seminary. I chose not to participate in that ceremony since it was predominantly geared to those men going on to be ordination and the ritual would itself reflect the very thing I decried in my project. So, I awaited the reception of the degree until it could be mailed. It would come to my new address as I was leaving shortly to take up residence in The Barn.

I was too excited to sit that late spring morning as I awaited the arrival of the moving truck that would transport my furnishings from the Women's Center to my new home outside Elk Lake, Wisconsin. The Barn was now a reality. Bill and I had finalized the deed and today I would move into my first home, albeit one with mixed functions. On my third cup of coffee I revisited the rooms of this present house to be sure I had all that belonged to me.

I needed a truck for the furniture and household furnishings donated by generous supporters from their basements or storage areas. I had scoured second-hand stores and garage sales for a while and gathered an interesting array of household essentials and some frills. The Barn was going to be so much fun to decorate. The previous owners left beds and a couple of occasional chairs. My friend, Regina, gave me a dining room set she used when she raised her three sons. It was a welcome addition. I had plants, of course, and a couple of pieces of furniture I purchased from the religious community that owned the house in which the Women's Center was located. I had some dishes and other kitchen items, enough to live in relative comfort. All of this needed to be gathered once the truck was here.

The formal dispensation papers had not yet arrived from Rome, but I knew they were forthcoming. I just couldn't wait. The canonical/legal paperwork that would release me from the obligations of the vows and officially separate me from the religious community was not that important to me. The severed relationship with the Order and the Church had occurred over a series of years.

"To be ourselves causes us to be exiled by many others, and yet to comply with what others want causes us to be exiled from ourselves." I jotted this quotation in one of my journal pages earlier, but I neglected to note the source. No matter, they were exactly the words I needed to review as I began this process of separation. They motivated me as I began the difficult task of informing family and friends of my forthcoming departure from religious life.

My sister, Lee, was the first one I told, after Bill, of course. She was aware of my growing dissatisfaction and my searching for a niche. We had talked in recent years about the male domination of the Church and the male God and its implications for us as women. She was not in the same place as I was. She continued to find her niche of comfort in parish ministry. She was teary, as I was, and expressed her preference that I not leave the Order. For the first time I shared with her more of the details of my relationship with Bill. She didn't seem surprised by my revelation, although we had not discussed it. In the end, she supported my decision. We talked about what my future might be and where I would live and work. Nothing had been clear at that point, but today she was coming to assist me in my move to The Barn.

My parents were the ones I was most reluctant to tell. Ironically, they were two of the most supportive. The three of us finished one of my mom's standard but tasty meals. It was not the most relaxed meal I remembered with them, but it went down rather easily.

"Mom and Dad, you know, I'm sure, that I've been having a difficult time with the Church and even with the direction of the Order. The dissolution of the Center is the final straw." I paused a moment, struggling for words that might best communicate my decision and make it as acceptable and understandable as possible for them. In that brief moment, I saw a look pass between them. They were not surprised, I thought, but almost relieved.

I told them of my meetings with Sarah and the decision I had reached to leave the Order.

Dad spoke first, "Marsha, you know we never tried to run the life of any of our children. We've always encouraged you to do the best you can, to make your own decisions and then to live with the results of those choices."

Mom said less but it was powerful. "We never knew why you went."

That was it, so much easier than I expected. I jumped from the table and gave each of them a big hug, delighted that they once again supported me in my choice. Even my dad had a few tears in his eyes, but we were all smiling.

"Do you want to live here until you can get a job and get settled?" That was Dad's concern.

Mom expressed her own. "We know how close you and Father Bill have been. He's a wonderful priest, and we think the world of him, but he is a little older than you. He might need care in a few years. Are you thinking of getting married?"

Her comment was interesting. I had not discussed the relationship with Bill in detail with my parents, but they knew we were very close friends. "No, maybe at some other time that might have been an option. It's really not what I want to do at this point. I'd only be leaving one kind of structure for another, and I want to have the freedom of being on my own. Bill is going through some changes, too. He's not eager to return to parish. We are both interested in spirituality and may try to develop a retreat center and work at that together."

Then I told them about the Barn, which we did not yet own, but hoped to, how we found it, and what it looked like. They both expressed an eagerness to see it although I could tell they had some apprehensions about my living in a barn! Mom eased the discomfort temporarily. "Jesus started in a barn."

Denise and Bob were enthusiastic about my decision as well. My brother, Francis, had died a few years earlier. I expected he, too, would have supported my change. In the course of his suffering through a rare disease over several years, we had some wonderful talks. As he sensed his life was drawing to a close at forty-seven, he talked with me one day as he reflected on the whole of his life. He had unmet expectations which he hoped to satisfy as he aged, but that was not to be. I held his hand at his bedside and lamented how he had wasted away physically. He had wonderful blue eyes, but they were glassy with medication now.

"Marsha, I'm not really afraid to die; the hardest part is the dying itself. I have a great family, my kids are good and I know they'll do fine. Barbara has been a super wife. I hope she'll find happiness again. I've had a good life."

While he didn't want to die, Francis felt good about how he lived and what he accomplished. Over the next months, I reflected on my own life and knew I would not feel the same when my time of death came unless I made some changes.

Now, the day of my departure is here. There is no group of well-wishers as there was on the day I joined the Order and on the many occasions when, as a beloved member, the community celebrated my contributions to the direction of the group. There is only my sister Lee and my friend, Lucille, wife and mother of four. I know many perceive me as a failure. I no longer care; my soul longs for peace and freedom. I am eager to seek new horizons.

I don't know what those horizons will be. I only know my immediate destination. The excitement is building in me; I have always loved visits to Wisconsin. Crossing the state line in the past allowed my soul to soar and my spirit to be at peace. Today was even more exciting. This was my home for the near future.

CHAPTER THIRTY

When the moving caravan of three cars and a truck arrived, Bill was waiting for us. He had spent the morning repairing the wooden walkway that led to the entrance of The Barn. He was concerned that someone might trip during the move. I was thrilled to see him but very concerned that he might hurt himself. He had experienced chronic back pain for several weeks by then, and it was only temporarily relieved by the pain medication he took every four hours. There he was, on his hands and knees, pounding planks into place so no one would get hurt.

"Bill, please be careful. We can always fix that entrance walk later," I said as I rushed to greet him.

He stood with some difficulty, held me tightly and said, "Welcome to your home. I hoped to finish this before you arrived."

Lee and Lucille hugged him and said how fascinating the place was. Lucille exclaimed with great enthusiasm, "What a great place this is, Bill. How did you two ever find it? We would have been lost if Marsha wasn't leading the way."

"It's a long story," he said and looked at me whimsically. I knew he was talking about more than the road to The Barn. His journey and mine had indeed been a long one, but we knew there was more to come. We were embarking on a new venture. For the moment that was in the forefront of our awareness. We would have to deal with whatever would develop with his cancer at another time. For the present, I was the only one, aside from medical persons, who knew he had cancer. That was his privacy need and I would respect it until it became intolerable. He wanted to believe he would be cured and so wanted to avoid any unnecessary attention from others if they discovered he battled cancer.

As Lee, Lucille and I moved to the door, Bill chatted with the movers. I crossed the threshold as though entering a sacred place. This was truly holy ground. A profound sense that I was "at home" for the first time in a very long time settled over me. It had been a rocky and treacherous road for some while, but I had finally arrived home.

I knew this was an emotionally mixed day for Lee, but she was supportive of my decision and happy to be involved in the transport. She had heard much about The Barn and was eager to see it for herself. We each knew we would no longer have in common the life we had shared as Sisters, although we would always be sisters.

My effervescent friend Lucille, was squealing with delight throughout the whole move. "Can you believe this space? What a great fireplace! Can I stay here sometimes? When are you going to have your first meeting? Wow! I can hardly believe this. Wait until I tell the others. They'll all want to come and stay here a while."

By mid-afternoon we had done as much as we could for the present. Lucille bade farewell and was still babbling excitedly as she drove down the long driveway to return home. Lee was going to stay overnight, and I was grateful because this was a big barn, and I felt just a bit apprehensive about being alone the first night.

Bill invited us to his home for supper so the three of us began the thirty-minute drive to Elk Lake. The late afternoon sun shone brightly on the Lake, highlighting the sail boats that lulled peacefully on the smooth water. This was a beautiful area, and I was thrilled to realize it was my neighborhood, so to speak.

When we returned to The Barn after a tasty supper and a celebratory evening, Lee told me how happy she was that I found such peace, and she hoped and prayed that would continue to grow and develop. We were both very tired physically and emotionally, so we went to bed fairly early.

The next morning, I rose with the sun, dressed quietly, and crept down the stairs to the kitchen where hot coffee simmered in the coffee maker. I had set the timer the night before so it would be available at the crack of dawn.

I slipped out the door to the "mud room" and my body cast a long shadow across it from the light of the skylight. The cows mooed in a near-by field. The rooster's call during the early morning hours alerted me to the fact that the neighbors had chickens and eggs, which they soon shared with me on a regular basis. The newly-cut hay on the hill teased my nose with its fresh, clean smell. *This just seems so unbelievable. Can it really be happening to me?*

After Lee came down stairs, saying how well she slept in the traffic-less quiet, we ate breakfast and she unpacked some boxes of books before returning to the city. As she made her way to the car, she stopped and took a sweeping look at the area. "It's really a peaceful and beautiful spot, Marsha. I'll be back often."

We hugged and fought tears that wanted to express the joy and sadness we felt. She drove slowly down the driveway and turned to wave once more before she exited to the main road. I returned inside and looked around the main floor. The move went well and took precious little time actually. The furniture had been arranged to give a semblance of order to the place. It was all very exciting.

In the next several weeks I settled into a more peaceful and prayerful mode than I experienced during the last months at Berakah Community. Those days were very difficult, and I was eager to put some of those painful memories behind me. It had been an unfortunate experience but as my dad so wisely told me, "It gave you the impetus you needed to make this change in your life."

The rhythm of the routine of those days was healing. I unpacked boxes, shelved books, hung pictures and reveled in my new freedom and peace. It was a thrill to wake up each morning in my own home. The Barn was isolated, though, and Bill felt I should keep Rosie with me. She was actually part of both of us. We inherited her from my sister Denise when she finished graduate school a few years earlier. We often rotated her from his living space to mine when either of us was away for retreats or vacations. Rosie was a Border collie mix who was very attached to both of us.

Within a short time, Bill and I established a routine for our days. We did not know where all this was all heading, but we knew we needed to plunge in and begin somewhere. The easiest place to start was outdoors. There were trees to trim, bushes to shape and flowers to plant. We made a conscious choice to delay the development of a vegetable garden until we could make the entire area more appealing.

Bill would arrive about 9:00 a.m. and receive a robust greeting from Rosie, who waited on the planks in front of the kitchen, staring down the driveway. We would then celebrate Eucharist and do our Centering Prayer. Initially, it was just the two of us, but gradually we began to draw others from the area. Afterwards, each of us would tackle an aspect of the grounds that we wanted to focus on for that day. We both thrived and the energy and enthusiasm we brought to the physical work seemed to dissipate the sexual tension we had experienced previously. It felt like we had found a niche, away from the scrutiny of those who would destroy what we were about.

CHAPTER THIRTY-ONE

It was a month or so before I heard from the Provincial. She called to tell me my papers had arrived from Rome. We set a date to meet and sign them. My life and activity at The Barn contributed to a tanned, relaxed and somewhat trimmed appearance. When I reached the door of the Provincial House, I felt my heart racing. I was eager to finalize the legal process but aware that this was closure on some significant aspects of my life. I had lived in this building for three years and worked here in leadership capacities for seven. Many memories lingered here.

My eyes filled with tears as I rang the bell and waited for the receptionist to open it. She led me to the familiar parlor where we would have the simple ritual signaling the end of one phase of my life and the beginning of another. I sat in this parlor many times before, often to process the separation of other members. I never expected to deal with my own dispensation in this place.

Sarah, the Provincial, was in the room. She stood and rushed to embrace me. After a bit, she held my shoulders and gently pushed me from her so she could look into my face and eyes. "You look good, Marsha, and very peaceful. Are you?"

"Yes, Sarah, I am. I feel relieved of the tension and strain that has been woven through my life these past years. I know it's initial euphoria, but I am very grateful for it."

Within a few minutes, my sister and three of my good friends arrived. Two of them were needed to witness the act of signing the formal papers, in addition to Sarah. The others wanted to support me because they cared for me and had been friends for a long time.

"Marsha, you look so good, tan and toned and rested. Are you just lying in the sun all day?" Grace's comment broke the tension as laughter filled the room. They all knew me too well—a workaholic and activist by nature. I then began to describe my days, working in the fields, clearing of tree limbs, and pruning bushes.

"You'll never believe my latest venture, though. For the first time in my life I am driving a garden tractor. That's the reason for the tan. I just love it. It offers such a great opportunity to reflect, at least now three weeks after I've learned to use it. Bill loves it, too, so we try to share our time on it."

Lee, who was the only one of the group who had seen The Barn, described her experience of it on moving day. "It's a wonderful place. The night I stayed in the guest room I was surprised to see that the ceiling was the top of the roof, many feet above the bed. At first, I wondered how well I would sleep in all that openness, but it was very special. I slept well. The grounds are wonderful, too, and I know Marsha and Bill will do a lot to shape them up as well."

There was a little more conversation and then Sarah invited us to begin the prayerful reflection prior to the formal signing of the papers. The prayer was taken from **MIRYAM OF JUDAH**.

Journeyer, it's time we renewed ourselves
Once we stood together at a bend in time,
but only for a moment.

Joy and pain mark our past.
But today I will look forward in hope:
Let us begin again.
We are responsible for what will be.
Responding, we construct new stories in our time.
Journeyer, is not now the time to travel,
To stand heart to heart as once we stood within
a bend in time?

We continued to share about the meaning of what was happening; it was moving and uplifting for me. I knew I left this group of friends with a sense of support and validation. We concluded with the signing of the documents, and then there were hugs and wishes of peace. We all enjoyed a pleasant lunch at a nearby restaurant where we told more stories. Finally, I set off for my new home. I felt so light hearted and eager to explore the meaning of this new phase of my life.

Bill was waiting at The Barn when I returned. I think he expected I would be terribly sad, and he wanted to be there for me. He was sitting on the bench outside the front door with Rosie, and they both showed their delight that I was back safe and sound. Bill stood gingerly, I thought, and held out his arms to receive me. "How did it go?"

"It went well, given the circumstances. Sarah led a special prayer service, and we shared stories and tears and laughter, too. It was hard for all of us, but perhaps a little less for me. I've been grieving this loss for a long time."

"I'm glad you're back. I was concerned all day, prayed on my tractor rounds for you. I thought that would be the best place to pass some of the time. It gave me something concrete to do and filled me with happy thoughts of you. I love watching you on that machine. It's one of my favorite images of you since we've been here."

We hugged again, each of us dealing with the significance of this day in our own way. I felt renewed, released and reenergized to pursue the path ahead. Bill was more somber, I thought, but neither of us chose to talk about what we felt at that time. The impact of my leaving the Order on his life was not clear, but it bothered him that I wasn't filled with remorse or guilt for having let people down. I didn't see it that way, knowing I could only be true to others if I were true to myself. Bill saw the disappointment of people as a major deterrent to making a change in his life. It was easier for him to live with the inconsistencies of his life than to embrace their consequences.

CHAPTER THIRTY-TWO

The preparation of the grounds continued throughout the summer. We thrived and enjoyed our new life. As his pain escalated more, he relied on pain pills every four hours. His own physical energy was affected, so he would often retreat to his own home in the mid-afternoon to nap. Generally, I would join him there and prepare supper for both of us after which I returned to The Barn.

About once a month, his good friend George, a fellow-priest, would come for a visit. Sometimes he and Bill would play golf and then the three of us would meet for dinner. George had not yet seen The Barn although he was aware of what we were trying to do. One of the times he came, he planned to stay with Bill over night, so I invited them to come for dinner at The Barn.

Up to now, Bill had managed to keep his cancer a secret, not even telling his family as he feared his sisters would be unable to handle the news. It became a burden for me, however, as living with the uncertainty of the future and the possibility that he might die began to wear on me. I suggested he begin to share his health concerns with a few close friends and that would allow me to make some contacts as well.

However, I was totally unprepared for what happened the night he and George arrived for supper after a fairly competitive round of golf. Their friendship dated back to their early days in the seminary. As so often happened with priests when they got together, especially if they were engaged in anything athletic, their conversation was either about their parishes and ministry or the competition they experienced when they golfed.

After dinner, we moved to the living room, and George continued to express his awe and delight at The Barn. He really felt it was a wonderful place for us to do the spirituality center. I think he was probably relieved that we would do something like that. I recall his dismay when I shared with him several months earlier my decision to leave religious life. He had such a concerned look on his face and gave Bill a penetrating and questioning glance. Bill simply added his support of my decision but offered no further discussion of it and whether this would alter his decision to remain a priest. I know George must have left there with prayers and Masses galore for Bill's continuing fidelity to priesthood.

When we relaxed in the living room, we continued the banter and then the conversation switched to what George was doing in ministry. Bill was becoming less and less able to participate in those conversations. He felt George was actually too tied up in that and didn't have enough life beyond ministry. Within a short time, he literally blurted out, "George, I have cancer and I'm not at all hopeful that I will be able to beat it. It is in the prostate and has begun to metastasize in my spine. Marsha is the only one who knows and I would ask you to keep this confidential, as well.

"When the time comes for my funeral, I would like you to be the celebrant and I want Marsha to preach the homily. She and I will plan the liturgy together. She is very good at that and knows what I value. In the meantime, we are going to continue our plans for this center in the hope that things do turn around, but I wanted to lay the groundwork with you."

George was stunned. He had been the sickly one throughout his life and fully expected Bill would celebrate his funeral liturgy. In fact, when they submitted their request for funeral and burial plans to the Archdiocese several years earlier, he asked Bill to be the celebrant. It seemed morbid to do that kind of planning so early, but the Archbishop wanted to avoid any unnecessary confusion about funeral plans at the time of a priest's death. Ironically, the year the request came from the Chancery for that information, Bill refused to consider anything about it. He expected to live a long time and didn't want to focus on his death at that point, so he never responded.

Now he felt like it might be necessary, and he wanted to avoid any conflict. He told George he would put it all in writing and give him a copy as well as the Chancery and his family. He would wait a while, though. He still wanted to keep this his secret. George knew his family well, and he didn't want them to know about it just yet.

If George was shocked, as I sensed he was, he didn't have too much to say. I, on the other hand, was totally blown away by Bill's revelation. We avoided talking about anything like this ourselves, and I burst into tears at the possibility that this was perhaps a closer reality than I had expected. In fact, I suspect Bill made the revelation because he had recently received an up-date on his prognosis from the urologist.

As the reality of his cancer began to register, Bill became discouraged, frustrated and angry, especially with the urologist. He admitted he might have missed the tumor in the previous exam because it could have been hidden from the x-ray he took at that time. That mistake allowed the tumor to grow and develop and metastasize.

"I thought he was a friend. He was no friend. I spent plenty of time with him when his wife was dying of cancer a year ago. When I needed him, he was nowhere to be found." Bill was irate.

This was a recurrent complaint dating to the time when the original diagnosis was made. Bill had made several attempts to reach him after that and always received the same message when he called his office.

"Doctor is not available today. I'll give him your message. What is your question, Father?"

Bill was interested in getting some sort of estimate on how much time he could expect, but he was unwilling to talk with the nurse about that. After several unsuccessful attempts to contact the urologist directly, Bill called a physician-friend on the staff of the same hospital to see if he could get an answer. When Jim called back, he told Bill he had some difficulty in contacting Dr. Jackson.

"He's been very scarce and unavailable at the hospital lately. He has a new baby now. I guess that's taking a lot of his time."

Bill was very surprised at that news since the doctor's wife died only a short time before, and he didn't realize the doctor had married his secretary, a much younger woman. He didn't mention the marriage to me when he called and said, bluntly and perhaps angrily, "Two years, Marsha. I just talked with Jim. He was finally able to reach Jackson. According to him, a person with cancer as rampant as mine would have no longer than two years."

Bill sounded calm, but I knew he was doing his best to control his emotions. My own response left me totally shaken. I didn't want to let him know that just now. I didn't trust myself to say much at all and what I did say was poorly chosen, I thought in retrospect.

"What do you want to do, Bill? Do you want to call The Barn quits and take some time to do things you enjoy?"

"Not at all. He could be wrong. I feel pretty good, except for the pain but the medication helps that. Let's just keep on doing what we're doing. Is that okay with you?"

"I think so."

When we hung up, I was filled with anxiety. *Two years! It's already been eight months since he told him. That means we are dealing with considerably less than two years.* My mind was reeling and my heart was pounding. *God, how much time does he really have?*

These past months had been wonderful. We worked very hard, prayed a lot and played a bit. Our daily routine continued to energize us, and we received a very favorable response from the people who came to the programs. They encouraged us so much. Even those in regular contact still had no idea of Bill's physical condition. They were looking for The Barn to continue for a long time.

We began to have Eucharist on Sunday mornings and persons came from Bill's previous parish, an hour's drive away, and some came from the local area. That was such a powerful experience for all of us. The ritual allowed greater intimacy of prayer and sharing. A community was beginning to build. It all seemed to be such a wonderful project. This new information stirred my darker self. *Why the hell did you think this would continue? You were having fun. You were happy. That's not supposed to last. Every time you get your hopes up, they get smashed. When will you stop dreaming? Get real!*

I paced and raged, my heart beating wildly and my eyes flooding with tears yet again. I was furious at myself for getting my hopes up. I was angry at Bill for getting sick, and I was frenzied once again at the institutional church that had made him sick. I knew I was behaving irrationally, but I didn't know what else to do. It was not a good morning, that cold January day when the world whirled out of control.

When Bill arrived some time later, we were still visibly shaken and frightened by the news that he had less than two years to live. Nothing else really seemed important — not the programs or the people or The Barn. It was all meaningless for the time being in light of his prognosis. We sat together, dazed and fearful. If only the doctor had leveled with us in the beginning, we might not have even begun. Now there was so much invested in The Barn. Each of us wanted desperately to succeed, to prove to our detractors that we were good and effective ministers. We longed for vindication. The urgency of Bill's situation filled us with a renewed energy to continue what we had begun.

We celebrated Eucharist and struggled to quiet ourselves enough to do Centering Prayer. At the end of that time, we sat again and pondered on our future course. At that moment, we both felt it was critical to continue.

CHAPTER THIRTY-THREE

Throughout the summer we concentrated on making the space more welcoming. By early fall, we felt ready to open the doors of The Barn to those seeking opportunities to pray and reflect in this peaceful environment. Our aspirations were not massive. We had no desire to become an institution, nor did we see ourselves in any way as a threat to the local Catholic Churches. Each of us came home to ourselves in a very important way, and we wanted to encourage others to continue on their own journeys so they might know greater freedom and peace in their daily lives. Bill and I recovered a missing link in our developing spirituality in nature—the patterns of life and death, the transformations as a result of seasonal changes. The tilling and sowing of grass and flowers brought us to a new realization of the connection between soul and body in the search for God.

The ominous threat of cancer was always with us, but somehow we maintained a level of peacefulness in our little corner of the world. We were removed from the scrutiny of those critical of our more liberal orientation and of our close friendship. They might well be continuing their criticisms, but we were not in the midst of it. We no longer confronted it on a regular basis, and it was wonderful and freeing. We knew with deep conviction that what we were about was Spirit-driven. Previous attempts we made in parish to promote and develop personal spirituality that was not exclusively linked to Mass and Sacraments had been thwarted.

Then, one Saturday morning, Bill arrived at the Barn for our shared activities. He looked concerned, I thought, his brow drawn into tight wrinkles, and his mouth was rigid. He was not smiling when he handed me the envelope he was carrying.

"This came in the mail yesterday. Read it and let's decide how we want to respond."

I noticed immediately the return address: Archdiocese of Waukesha, The Chancery, and Administrative Headquarters. My heart pounded. Of course the envelope was only addressed to Bill, leaving me to speculate whether it was just personal to him or whether in fact it had to do with our center.

"What's it about, Bill?" I was reluctant to open the envelope.

"Open it and read it yourself." He was irritable and edgy and that was a clue as to the contents. Reluctantly, I removed the letter from the envelope and read:

"Dear Father Creed,

It has come to our attention that you are engaged in spiritual activity that has not been approved through this office. At your earliest convenience, I would like to have a meeting with you to discuss this matter. Please call and schedule an appointment.

Sincerely in Christ, Father Alphonsus Schultz."

I tossed the letter on the table and shouted, "Damn! Are we never to have any peace? We're not doing anything wrong. Why can't they leave us alone? Apparently it's not possible to escape the long arm of the institution." I was pacing rapidly and furiously around the floor.

"Don't get too excited, Marsha. It might just be a friendly invitation to share what we are doing," Bill said in an attempt to smooth my ruffled feathers.

"I doubt that. Someone has probably called to complain about what we're doing. Who can it be? Surely those who are coming to the liturgies and workshops wouldn't do that. They are so involved and supportive. It's probably one of those pastors who are threatened by us. Remember, none of them even responded to our letter and phone call offering to meet with them and their staffs to see if and how we could collaborate with them."

Bill was not interested in pursuing the source of the complaints. We were fed up with the suspicion and mistrust and negative energy generated by that kind of speculation in the past. He went to the phone and dialed the Chancery number on the letterhead. Although it was Saturday, he made immediate contact with the writer. We learned later that he was there on Saturday because he was leaving for vacation the following day.

"Father Alphonsus Schultz speaking."

"Good morning, Father. I'm Father Bill Creed. I received your letter and am calling to schedule an appointment to describe what we're doing and talk about your concerns."

"Sure, Father, but I'm leaving town for a couple of weeks tomorrow. Let's set a date for when I return. How about February fourteenth at nine thirty a.m.?"

"That's fine. Of course, I am working very closely with Marsha Malone, and I want her to participate in this conversation. She has been vitally involved in the formation of this spirituality center."

"Okay, bring her."

Bill and I tried to stifle our anxiety and the uncertainty generated by the prospect of the meeting, still three weeks away, but it was always lurking in the background, somewhat near the cancer threat. Was this another dead end for us? Suppose he told us we would have to discontinue our work. My new status as a lay person gave me a greater measure of freedom. Bill, on the other hand, was much more vulnerable to the decision that would be made following our conversation.

When the day arrived, we left early so we would arrive in plenty of time for our meeting. The Chancery Office was about an hour and ten minutes away, housed in a large, modern building of blond bricks and glass doors and windows. We parked the car and walked toward the entrance to the rambling structure across from Lake Michigan. We negotiated a series of long hallways until we found the office of Father Alphonsus. I felt like I was trapped in a maze. Upon entering the outer office, Bill was greeted by the three women seated in the reception area.

"Good morning, Father."

I looked above and around me in a statement without words. I knew I had not physically disappeared, but there was no acknowledgement of my presence by these ladies. One of them walked to the door of the summoner's office and said, "Father Creed is here."

Once again I looked for some indications that I was still embodied and pinched my arm. Yes, I was still here. Bill stepped aside to allow me to enter the room, and I was finally greeted with, "You must be Marsha."

I answered, "I am Marsha Malone."

The priest who occupied the office was munching a cookie. "I'm just finishing a Valentine's cookie. Do you mind?"

We assured him we did not object as he seated us at a round table surrounded by comfortable chairs. He moved to another section of his office where an oversized mahogany desk contained a plate with a few more cookies. Father picked up the one he was eating and walked toward us, crumbs falling to the floor. It was perfect for me. Father ate his cookie as he was about to make some determination about our future.

Alphonsus was well groomed, wearing a top-of-the-line clerical suit, impeccable white shirt adorned with striking cufflinks, and elegant shiny black shoes. He was well tanned, indicating his time away had been spent in a warm and sunny climate. Most of his attention was directed to Bill. He looked at me only when I offered a comment or explanation about what we were doing and why.

"Well, Father, the reason I called you is because of the concern the Archbishop has about small groups that are springing up all across the Archdiocese. He believes we should be doing all we can to build up the parishes rather than diverting people from them."

"Alphonsus, these people are not participating in parishes at this time," I interjected.

Defensively, he queried, "But why aren't they? We should encourage them to reconcile with their parishes. There is a need for community."

"Yes, Alphonsus," I said, "and that is what we are offering them." I refused by now to call any of the clergy "Father" or to address them as "Reverend." Those were categories of their own making and continued to perpetuate the notion of a masculine God and the patriarchal system that was so painful to me.

Apparently I touched a nerve with my last comment as he gave me a slanted glance, followed by, "They should be finding it in their own parishes."

I could feel some tension building in Bill as he shuffled in his chair and crossed his leg. No doubt, he feared a potential confrontation between us. He broke in quickly.

"They are not involved in parishes at this time, Father. I know from my recent pastoral experiences that some people are looking for more than they can find in their parishes. If your concern is that we'll take people away from the local churches, let me assure you that we have a very small gathering space. We have no room for more than twenty or twenty-five participants on a given Sunday. I don't think we are a threat to existing parishes in the area."

"We'd love to have you join us some Sunday, meet the people

we serve and see what we are doing. I feel sure it will put your concerns to rest," I said with as much enthusiasm as I could muster. He offered no response but proceeded to address Bill. "Three of the local pastors have expressed their fears that you might take people from them." I think I knew which three they were. The bottom line was the fear that people would shift their contributions to The Barn and away from the parishes.

The Chancellor continued his lecture about the archbishop's concern for orthodoxy in small groups. He felt confident, after talking with us, that what we were doing was fine. He turned in his chair so he could focus his attention exclusively on Bill.

"Father Creed, I have done some checking about you and find that you are a priest in good standing in the Archdiocese of Chicago. Therefore, I would like to give you faculties to minister in Waukesha."

I thought that was an insult and would have addressed it had he checked on me. Bill chose not to pursue that. I knew the remainder of the conversation would in no way include me so I began to distract myself by looking across the top of the shelves that lined the room. There was an impressive array of golf trophies from various parts of the country. *No wonder he's so tan.* I then overheard Alphonsus' words as I reviewed the geography of the trophies.

"Giving you faculties, Father, means that you can say Mass in the Archdiocese and hear confessions. You can't perform marriages, though, without the permission of the local pastor because it is his responsibility to marry a couple. If you get his permission, you can perform a marriage ceremony. You can forgive sins, except that which is reserved to the archbishop, the sin of abortion."

I entered the conversation now because I couldn't stand the way things were going. "What does that mean, Alphonsus?"

"That means if a woman comes to confession and seeks forgiveness for having an abortion, the priest would have to withhold absolution until he could check with the archbishop. He is the only one who can forgive the sin of abortion."

I could hardly believe what I was hearing. I counseled women who struggled with their decision to have an abortion. They were terrified to approach the confessional while trying to come to some peace with themselves, God and/or the Church. How would the priest react? They were very fearful and apprehensive. How would they feel when told to come back the next week to see if the archbishop forgave them? That was absurd!

"If you've ever been involved with a woman who had an abortion, Alphonsus, I trust you would see the absurdity of what you are suggesting about forgiveness," I stammered. Again, only a look from him, no response.

When we finally finished, I managed to bid farewell to the cookie priest, calmly and demurely, but I wanted to run from his office and the building screaming. As we passed through the outer office, Bill was bid adieu by the same three ladies, and we started down the cavernous hallway. I exploded. As the pitch and tenor of my voice escalated in the hollow, empty corridor, I was happily surprised to see Bill expressing his reaction. His voice was quiet, but his naturally ruddy complexion was almost beet red, and he began to pound the tiled floor with his shoes. His forty years of priesthood had not prepared him for today, I knew.

We reached the parking lot, and I shouted to the heavens as though my voice might somehow alert the universe to the terrible injustices perpetrated through this institution. I threw my hands above my head, turned to Bill and cried, "Do you believe what just happened?"

He was so clearly irritated. In the past, whenever my outrage at the institutional injustice of the Church was expressed, he tried to understand and support me. He often agreed with me but still held out hope for the conversion of the institution. Today he seemed in a new place.

"Marsha, when he said he wanted to give me faculties, I didn't know what he was talking about. I thought he wanted me to teach in a college somewhere. I haven't heard that in years."

We drove home in relative silence, aware that each of us was becoming less connected to the institutional church, even though we now had its "approval" to continue what we were doing, or at least Bill did. I didn't matter to them any more, but I knew with a renewed clarity why I had made the decision to leave religious life and institutional ministry.

CHAPTER THIRTY-FOUR

The winter was upon us and Wisconsin can be harsh with lots of snow, ice and bitter cold. We continued our Sunday Eucharist and the weekly programs. The formal papers designating Bill as legitimate in the Archdiocese arrived a few weeks after our meeting. It was supposed to hang in a prominent place in The Barn for all to see. We chose to tuck it in a file cabinet in the event we might need it at a future date. We did not need to display it. We spent considerable time alone and together developing ideas and insights for new programs, reading about new directions in spirituality as well as cancer. We continued to carry on as though a long future awaited us, but by the time early spring arrived, we knew this was not likely.

Winter seemed to last forever, and we were eager to return to the yard where we could work out some of our feelings and concerns as we tilled the soil and continued to spruce up the grounds. That was short-lived, however. Bill went for his monthly blood test and learned that the Lupron was not working. His PSA count was rising. He knew something was changing because he was experiencing increased and more frequent pain in his back and shoulders. The pain medication was not lasting more than an hour or so. Chris Kolb, his Wisconsin doctor, suggested he begin radiation treatment in late May.

That altered the pattern of our days considerably. Bill would arrive in the morning, and we would celebrate Eucharist and do Centering Prayer. On the days when we held some other program, we would often be joined by several others. People from Bluff Lakes continued to say how wonderful he looked. They still had no clue of the devastation that was playing havoc with his spine. Chris arranged for the initial interview with the oncologist and suggested we take the limousine from the hospital parking lot for the first trip.

We arrived at the hospital a little early to be sure we could locate the proper parking lot and the designated limousine. The local cancer patients always traveled to a larger facility in a nearby city. For some this was a hardship until Jeanette, the owner of an Exotic Dance Club in the town, contributed the services of a driver and a limo to take them to and from the treatment site. Bill contacted Tony, the driver, and ascertained there was room for both of us. He told Bill I could only go with him in the limo the first time since space was reserved for cancer patients only.

We approached the limousine and found three other people already in the vehicle. After brief introductions, we settled into a strained silence. Once we were all accounted for, Tony started the vehicle and we were on our way. Neither Bill nor I knew the route we would take, either in terms of the drive or the radiation treatments. After being on the road about fifteen minutes, we stopped outside a dilapidated farmhouse.

"We always stop here to pick up Adam. He has no way to get to the hospital parking lot," Marge said.

As we watched, we saw a man emerge from the house. Slowly, aided by a walker, Adam made his way down the unpaved driveway to the limousine. Tony assisted him into the empty seat across from the rumble seats on which Bill and I rode. Tony stowed Adam's walker in the trunk. Adam's wonderfully worn face bore the signs of a life-time on a Midwestern farm. His bushy snow-white hair was as refreshing as a snow capped mountain in the hot summer. His generous smile revealed a mouth minus several teeth, but his smile was engaging nonetheless. Everyone greeted Adam, and he had a word for each of them.

He looked at Bill and then at me, as if to determine who was the patient. His gaze focused on Bill. "Haven't seen you before. This your first trip? What kind of cancer you got?"

The directness of his question thrust us immediately into an awareness we were trying to deny. Perhaps Adam's forthrightness disarmed Bill somewhat because he was normally very guarded when it came to naming and discussing his disease.

"I have prostate cancer. It's moved into my spine."

"Oh," he said, "mine's liver and lung. I've been going for about three months now. I'm lucky they're willing to stop by for me or I'd have no way to get to the treatments."

"Are they making a difference?" Bill asked

"I don't think so, but they tell me I'd have much more pain without the treatments. I've been using the walker for the past two and one half months."

That opened the conversation for the other passengers. Marge, who was accompanying her husband, Matt, began, "Matt has Alzheimer's as well as bone cancer. He can't make the trip alone because he gets so confused and that's why I get to ride along."

She made it sound like an opportunity for a pleasant outing, but her face betrayed the pain and anxiety she was experiencing. Her husband smiled but his eyes remained vacant. She told us he had no idea what was going on most of the time.

The third passenger, Rita, was very thin and pale and looked quite ill. She admitted with some reluctance that she battled uterine cancer, and then retreated into silence. It was a rather somber trip.

After a bit, Marge said, "This should be our last week. We've been coming all through the winter. I'm sure glad it's almost over. Some days I was afraid we'd never make it with all the snow."

Bill and I shot a horrified look at each other.

"You came five days a week?" he asked.

"Yes, every day but Saturday and Sunday. Weekends are off."

We had no idea what to expect in terms of treatment, but we were certainly not prepared for this trip five days a week.

"You've been coming since February?" Bill asked. "That seems like such a long time. How is that determined?"

"It depends upon the size, number and location of the tumors. Sometimes we take three weeks at a time followed by a break of a week or so. Other times we came every day for six weeks."

Oh my God! I was very unsettled with that information and filled with apprehension. I knew Bill was upset as well because he retreated into a deep silence. When we arrived at the Cancer Treatment Center we entered a large waiting room occupied by almost twenty persons in varying stages of the disease. Some looked ravaged, others not noticeably afflicted. People smiled as the new group entered. A few exchanged up-dates on how they were doing.

Finally, we went into the office of the oncologist who would determine the course of Bill's treatment. He was a charming man with a crisp British accent and a witty sense of humor, which we appreciated at that point. Bill's first question, as we viewed the wall of x-rays that shone back at us, was how much time the treatments might take. We could see, even with our unprofessional eye, that there were tumors everywhere.

"Well, looking at these pictures, I can tell you I've seen better and I've seen worse--more better than worse. We'll start where the pain is most invasive and go from there. Do you want to begin treatment today? I think it would be a good idea. I suspect you are having a great deal of pain."

"Might as well begin as long as we're here," Bill said.

Then followed a discussion about the most stressful source of pain, and it was decided to begin with Bill's chest. He was led to a treatment room, and I returned to the waiting room. Adam was finished with his treatment for the day. He looked at me with a reassuring smile, "What did they say? How long will it be?"

"They think six weeks for this first round, but there are so many tumors, and they are still developing. The doctor said he'd be coming quite a while."

"Oh." That was enough for him to reach his own conclusion about Bill's future, it seemed. In fact, Bill's treatment plan was lengthy. After the first six weeks, he had a brief respite and then began another series of six-week episodes. Through the summer months of treatment, Bill was able to drive himself to the limo where he met several new people. There was always a turnover in riders. Some left the limousine group with hope. "They think they've got it all." Others left sadly. "They said there's nothing more they can do."

For the first two rounds of radiation, Bill felt well enough to ride in the limousine. Gradually, the treatments and the travel and the waiting for the others became too much for him. The pain he normally experienced was exacerbated by the movements the technicians made to position him on the table in the treatment room. When the third round of visits was ordered, I assumed the responsibility for driving him directly to and from the Treatment Center. He was extremely grateful, and I was actually relieved to accompany him. It was a difficult wait every afternoon until he would return.

By late August, the oncology staff conferred and suggested he take time off until or whenever the pain erupted. There was no longer any doubt about the fact that they considered his cancer terminal. Many new tumors appeared in the skeletal system, but for the moment they were not causing pain. We bid farewell to the staff, all of whom had been so kind and gracious and caring. We set off for home, grateful for the fact that we would not have to make this trip for a while. We soon learned it would be a very short respite.

CHAPTER THIRTY-FIVE

We were happy to have the extra free time. The trips to the Cancer Treatment Center generally took most of the afternoon. We tried once again to return to the work at hand, continuing the outreach of The Barn and working the land. Bill's energy was significantly diminished, but as long as he was not in pain, he continued to do what he could in preparing the grounds.

We set aside a Saturday in early September to communicate to the people on our mailing list the programs we hoped to offer for the fall and winter seasons. We had completed almost a year of activity at The Barn and were really encouraged to develop and expand the programs. While involved in that activity, we could put the concern about cancer out of the forefront of our consciousness, and we imagined we would have lots more time to develop what we had begun.

Bill received a letter confirming his certification to lead Centering Prayer Retreats. His internship was completed. Several days later, a letter from the Cardinal contained his formal assignment to the ministry of spiritual leadership at The Barn. Those pieces were all in place and gave him a tremendous feeling of accomplishment.

He had agonized about that meeting with the Cardinal. He wanted to have The Barn ministry recognized as his assignment. Perhaps he thought it would also validate the ministry there in the event he would be unable to continue because of his health. He rehearsed his strategy with me a few times once a designated meeting date was set.

"Marsha, I really believe what we're doing is very good and worthwhile. I want it to stand on its own merits. I don't think I'll tell the Cardinal about my cancer. I don't want that to influence his decision. I don't want to be assigned to this ministry because I'm sick."

"Bill, I understand what you're saying, but I think you have to tell him about your health conditions. He should hear it from you."

"You're probably right. I think I'll wait until the conversation about The Barn is over and then tell him when I'm ready to leave."

"It's your decision, Bill. Tell him however you want, but I think he should know from you."

It was very important to him that he be assigned to The Barn. He didn't just want to do it on his own. In some ways, he had moved so far from the trappings of priesthood, but there were some places he was held by a tight cord. That was one of the reasons we could never marry. He could live with limited peace with our relationship, but was unable to think of himself as anything but a priest. Even when the vitality and hope he experienced as a result of our deep loving friendship manifested itself in wonderful ways, he was plagued by the fear that he would be nothing if he left and would not function very well.

We continued our planning and drafting of the letter to the supporters of The Barn throughout the morning. I sensed his apprehension at the physical toll the cancer was taking on him. It exceeded the worst of our dreads. At the same time, he mustered all the energy and determination he could to make this work. After finalizing the schedule, I planned to type it and have it ready for the printer on Monday.

Bill seemed particularly exhausted and depressed when we stopped for lunch. He ate a bit and then went to lie down. It occurred to me that a nice rib dinner, cooked on the grill, might be a fitting close to a successful morning of planning and would perhaps cheer him a bit. In spite of the pain and medication he was taking his appetite remained pretty solid. So, while he slept, I went to the store and carried on like life was "normal," but my heart was heavy and my anxiety level was off the charts. I was filled with apprehension as I wandered through the aisles of the market, looking at people and wanting to shout, "Do you know what's happening to Bill? To me? To us?"

Their lives appeared just fine while I had the implicit sense mine was about to crumble. When I returned home, I went to the door of his room and knew from his steady breathing that he was sleeping soundly. The pain medication contributed to that, dulling the sharpness of the stabbing attack on his bones. While he slept, I began the preparation of the ribs, without much enthusiasm. Actually, I had little desire for them and suspected he would not want much either, but it seemed important to continue as though life was moving in an orderly fashion. It lent stability and security to the passage of days, although it was clearly peripheral.

When Bill emerged from his room several hours later, he looked drawn and quite distressed. As he came toward me, I noticed more ominous changes. He walked with difficulty and appeared more stooped. The ruddiness had long since left his cheeks, and his blue eyes lost their luster, dulled by pain and medication.

"Marsha, I don't know what's going on. I've never had this much pain. I can't stand it any longer."

I realized he was pushing some new limits, so I went to the phone and dialed his physician's on-call number. Fortunately, Chris was taking call that evening. I was so relieved to hear his voice that my own voice cracked with my tears. "Chris, it's Marsha. Bill is having a terrible day. The pain seems excruciating. Nothing we've tried has given him any respite."

"Marsha, take him right to the emergency room. We have to do something about that pain right away. I'll call and tell them to expect you."

As I made preparations for that trip, Bill suggested we at least try the ribs since I had spent so much time on them. That was so like him, however, I could have choked on the one I ate as I was fearful and anxious about what was happening and what this might mean for the future. He sampled one, and we left for the emergency room.

They were expecting us and began immediately to attack the source of the pain, giving him injections and intravenous insertions that didn't even touch the source. They sent us home with additional medications, but I felt less than hopeful about his finding any relief. If the drugs they injected didn't help, how would these pills by mouth do any good? I decided to stay at his home that night. I couldn't leave him alone. Neither of us slept much. He got up several times during the night to try to walk off the pain and I walked with him. He had no relief, no matter how many of the pain pills he took.

When Sunday morning broke, he was still in a great deal of pain. We were both very tired, but we needed to return to The Barn for Mass. It was difficult, but there was no way to notify people, some of whom were probably already on their way. It was obvious to all who came that he was suffering, but he was still unwilling to share his health situation with anyone else at that time. So, friends who gathered there left with the belief that he had seriously wrenched his back. Always, his privacy was the priority and he did not want any outpouring of sympathy. A few offered suggestions of alternative ways to minimize the pain, but for him all of that seemed impossible to even consider.

We toughed it out that day as we had so many days before. We tried in vain to relieve the pain. The medication was impotent. It and the subsequent radiation treatments were successful up to now, but this was a very different time. When Chris called later that day and learned of the difficulty we experienced, he suggested we come to his office first thing in the morning.

He was waiting for us and escorted us directly into his office rather than to the exam room. His concern was evident and the urgency in his voice was alarming. He ascertained the major pain source after talking with Bill and guided him for one more set of x-rays. As he exited the office, he turned to me and said, "Marsha, I hate this disease."

I felt as though I had been stabbed in the heart. His comment said much more than I wanted to hear. As I waited alone in the tiny office, my mind raced wildly and my imagination filled with worse-case scenarios, possible implications and ominous future consequences. The room was too small for me to pace, but I remember wanting to run and shout and pound on the walls.

When they returned to the office, I was shocked to see how stooped and labored Bill's walking was. Just the movement necessary for the x-rays aggravated his condition. Chris showed us the x-rays and pointed out where the cancer was spreading. His sense of helplessness was evident. He really cared and was very frustrated at his inability to change anything. He looked at us intensely and compassionately.

"I don't like the way this is spreading. We're going to have to do something about the pain immediately. I'll call and arrange for you to begin another round of radiation today. That seemed to give you some relief before. I think you should consider the possibility of getting involved with hospice. There's a really good group here. It'll be helpful to get those supportive relationships in place."

We were stunned. Our eyes met and tears began to flow. Apprehension and fear filled us, but we told Chris we'd be able to take care of things for now. He scheduled a radiation treatment, and we left immediately for the Cancer Center. The trip, the pain and the treatment process exhausted Bill and all he wanted was to go to bed and try to sleep when we got home. We talked briefly about hospice but neither of us wanted to take that step; people only called in hospice when the situation was hopeless and the end was near. We weren't ready to admit that just yet.

The next morning, Chris called again to check on Bill and me. His concern for both of us was always evident, and I was so grateful to him for that. He again suggested we contact hospice. Reluctantly, we both agreed and the next day, we met with Jolyn for the first time. She was the hospice coordinator and the woman who had founded it in our area. Jolyn was wonderful and spoke so compassionately and sensitively. We both liked her immediately. While she was there, it was necessary to make a decision about who would be the contact person during this time. There wasn't a doubt in his mind—or mine.

From that day on, I was Bill's designated caregiver, responsible for his health care and responsive to hospice for his well-being. After all the years of struggle with our relationship, I was the person who would be with him daily for the remainder of his life. It all seemed so natural, but also so very painful. After years of soul-wrenching questions and decisions about our relationship, we were finally, publicly together.

What irony.

What tragedy.

CHAPTER THIRTY-SIX

For the first month or so, Bill seemed comfortable with the pain management hospice provided and the continued radiation treatments, and we began to fantasize that he was getting better. Actually, I think it was his fantasy more than mine. I was seeing changes in weight and more loss of stamina which he was unaware of, unable or unwilling to acknowledge. On one level, he sought to maintain some sort of normal functioning but his energy, strength and drive were significantly diminished.

We continued the Centering Prayer sessions once a week and the Sunday liturgy. By now, people from his previous parish were aware of his health crisis and the number of participants increased dramatically. Many more than usual drove from Illinois to see him for perhaps one more time. The stress of all of that became too much for both of us, especially Bill, and we finally acceded to the aggression of the disease and canceled all public celebrations. Bill became increasingly weaker and more depressed. I did my best to provide a positive and supportive presence, keeping my own fears and panic from him most of the time. People were kind and generous with their time, but it was an incredibly lonely journey.

On occasional days, Bill was not scheduled for radiation and seemed to have a resurgence of energy. On those few days we tried to do something special. One beautiful October day, I suggested to him that we take a drive. He didn't usually want to do much traveling as we spent so much time in the car for the five days per week trip for radiation.

"Bill, it's such a beautiful day. How about going to Lake Michigan? I've heard there's a really nice park right near the water. Today is mild enough for us to sit outside. On the way back, we can stop for lunch if you feel like it."

He agreed and we set off together with Rosie. When we arrived at the park, Bill bolted out of the car with his cane, a recent necessary support, and he began to scurry across the boulders to get closer to the water. I became concerned and hollered to him. "Bill, please be careful! You could slip and fall and create more problems. Please slow down."

He shouted back over his shoulder, "What difference does it make?"

I really didn't know what was driving him, but I know I was fearful. For a fleeting moment, I wondered if he would plunge into the water. He seemed to have thrown caution to the wind as he scampered across the top of the boulders. Soon, fatigue struck with all its vehemence and he returned to the car haltingly and with a new frailty.

Our return trip was quiet. Bill seemed somber, as though a new level of reality was making its presence known. As we neared Elk Lake, Bill suggested we stop for lunch. I was reluctant, but he insisted it would do us good to have a break.

When we stopped he was so irritable and impatient with the waitress that I was quite uncomfortable. That was so unlike him. We ate hurriedly, leaving lots on our plates. He went to the car while I paid the bill and apologized to the waitress. That was our last excursion except for the rides to and from the hospital for the continuation of radiation.

Except for the regular visits from hospice personnel, our life became much more private and we settled into coping with the disease and celebrating the time we had, even as his terminal condition became more obvious. The pain in his back was impossible to contain, and he could not tolerate it. Through a friend who was a gynecologist he learned of a new treatment, used in child-birth but being experimented with for serious back pain in other situations. The insertion of the morphine epidural was effective for the pain, but it gradually began to take a toll on Bill's mental and emotional condition. He was subject to frequent memory lapses, profound confusion and serious disorientation. One day, he came into the living room where I was reading and asked, "Marsha, who am I? Am I a coach?"

"You used to be a coach, Bill. You worked with lots of girls and boys in volleyball and basketball. You're not a coach now, Bill. You're my friend and a priest."

"Thanks, I've been wondering about that." With that he ambled back toward his room where he resumed his musings. It broke my heart to see the dissolution of his faculties. He seemed always to know me and often expressed gratitude for the care I was giving him. One day when his friend, George, was visiting, he told him about the care I gave him.

"George, Marsha has done a great job. If anybody says anything about her after I'm gone, please tell them she has been a great friend and has taken excellent care of me. I don't know where I would have been without her."

With very few words, George said he was aware of the excellent care Bill was receiving. He didn't know why anyone would have anything to say. George always seemed comfortable in our presence, although Bill never really talked about all the dimensions of our friendship and had no idea how George would feel if he knew all the facts.

My decision to leave religious life was influenced by the archaic perception of the Church that one cannot truly minister effectively unless one is celibate. Our experience confirmed that our loving each other contributed to the richness of our service to others.

CHAPTER THIRTY-SEVEN

The week before Christmas, Bill had an evaluation with the oncologist. He suggested we continue with the radiation. While he was not experiencing pain, the doctor showed us x-rays once again that indicated the presence of tumors that would soon be impinging on nerves and would numb Bill's left arm. He wasn't sure when that might happen, but felt it was important to begin radiation on that site as soon as possible.

Neither of us said much on the drive home. We were both so weary of the relentless routine of the treatments. I was lamenting the inevitability of more of the same, wishing we could just have a more peaceful waiting period. By now we both knew our days together were coming to an end. About halfway home, Bill broke the silence.

"Marsha, what do you think about continuing radiation?"

"Bill, that's up to you. I'll do whatever you think is best for you."

"Well, I think if numbness is the consequence, there won't be the pain. I don't think we'll be going back for radiation. I can live with numbness, I think."

I was relieved for the moment. Christmas was approaching —our last one together—and I hoped we could have some quieter time without that daily trip. We never did return for more radiation. There was no longer the need to try to shrink the ravaging tumors. The pain was being managed with the morphine epidural.

The Sunday before Christmas all of Bill's family came to visit: his sisters, nieces, nephews, grand-nieces, and grand-nephews. I decorated the house to give a festive air, and we all enjoyed the luncheon they brought. Everyone's heart ached at the prospects of what would come before too long, but we managed to have a pleasant celebration.

On Christmas Day, my family came to The Barn where Bill and I joined them for dinner. I invited his sister to join us and arranged for my sister to pick her up on the way as they lived rather close to each other. Bill was especially pleased to have her included although he knew she would bring tension; however, she was his only unmarried sister and he felt somehow responsible for her. That, too, was a pleasant time. Everyone, of course, was happy to see both of us. We didn't stay long, as he was very tired, but we ate dinner and then returned to his home, the three of us.

One of the gifts of hospice was the availability of persons to assist with care of the patient and provide some opportunities for the care-giver to have a respite. I really didn't want to have too much time away, but it was becoming more difficult to leave him alone as he was often confused and subject to falls. One of the aides would come twice a week to bathe him, which was very hard for him to endure. He hated being tended to so personally, but it was essential and he cooperated as best he could.

Once again, we seemed to have settled into a bit of a predictable routine. For Bill it was a special gift as his greatest desire was that he be able to die in his own home. My presence and the assistance of the hospice personnel allowed that to happen, until the night he experienced an extremely aggressive reaction to the accumulated morphine in his system.

He went to bed, I hoped for the night, when he suddenly appeared at the front door, in his pajamas, and announced he was going to catch the bus. He wanted to go somewhere and there was nothing I could do to dissuade him. He pushed me against the wall when I tried to stop his exit. I was frightened and reached for the phone and dialed hospice.

"Bill is out of control tonight. He is aggressive and is planning to leave the house. He's very confused. I tried to give him the sedatives, but he pushed them from my hands. Can you come?"

"We'll be right there. Try to keep him there if you can."

I don't know how I did manage to restrain him, because when the nurses arrived they gave him two shots to calm him— the first didn't take. Eventually, they took him from his home to the hospital and assured me they would contact me as soon as they had him settled. I should wait until the next morning to visit.

I was terrified and maintained little confidence that he would return to his home. After all this time of enduring the ravages of the disease, he would not be home when he died, and I would probably not be with him. That felt cruel to me, and I expressed my feelings to the nurse when she called to tell me he was settled. She reassured me that he was probably not going to die within the next few days, and he could probably come back home again.

The next morning when I arrived at his room, Bill was strapped in his bed. He had become very restless during the night, and they were afraid he would fall. He greeted me warmly and seemed to have absolutely no remembrance of the circumstances that brought him to the hospital. After several days, in consultation with the doctor, hospice staff, and me, Bill was allowed to return home where he was confined to the hospital bed we had obtained several months earlier. For his convenience and accessibility to the persons who visited him, we agreed to place the bed in the living room. It would also allow him to engage in whatever activity he chose. One of the things he loved was watching the snow fall and the birds feeding from his living room window.

The day he returned from the hospital, I hired Lydia to sit with him through the night so that I could get some rest. She was wonderful and offered comfort and reassurance to both of us. If he was restless, she would tend to him, and I could try to sleep with greater ease. She was an invaluable aide, referred to us by hospice. She would arrive at 10:00 p.m. and leave at 6:00 a.m.

He was disengaged from much of what was happening in the world, but occasionally he would look at the TV for news or perhaps a glimpse of a story he used to enjoy. It was clear to me that he was releasing his hold on life. He rarely talked about The Barn, which had receded into the background of both our consciousnesses.

We prayed often and began a ritual every evening. I asked him if he would like to be anointed, and he readily expressed a desire for me to do that. So, each night, I would sign his head, heart, mouth, and shoulders asking for peaceful thoughts, a calm heart, a mouth to praise, and a body free of pain. At the end of the brief blessing, he would say, "That's beautiful."

CHAPTER THIRTY-EIGHT

Bill's "active dying" began exactly a week after his return from the hospital. Julie bathed him and he seemed comfortable and restful. George, who had visited weekly since September, arrived for his visit. He had been Bill's faithful friend for all their years of seminary and beyond, and he was particularly attentive to him during this trial. In fact, he was the only priest Bill wanted to see during his illness.

When George arrived, Bill was alert and exchanged a few words, but he seemed more tired and listless than usual. George was fairly uncomfortable with Bill's physical diminishment. George had been in frail health for years and fully expected the robust, athletic Irishman to outlive him. As we stood beside his bed, Bill suddenly turned his attention and gaze from George to me and said pathetically, "Marsha, why doesn't God take me? I've been asking Him for so long, but He just doesn't seem to hear me."

"Bill, maybe you ought to ask Her. You might get the answer you're waiting for."

We had been over the gender-of-God ground over many years, and I knew Bill would appreciate the humor, as sick as he was. He smiled weakly and said, "I'll try that." His own convictions about the use of exclusive masculine language for God had grown. It became fairly routine for him to address God as Father and Mother in his public and private prayers and reflections.

George and I moved the few feet to the table for the lunch I prepared. This was the ritual we developed during the time Bill was actively fighting the disease. George arrived in the late morning and the three of us would talk. While I prepared lunch, the two of them could talk. After lunch, the conversation continued until George left to return to the city.

While we ate, I was distracted as George talked about his parish and other church-related activities. I stole many glances toward the hospital bed that held the cancer-ravaged body of my beloved friend. I was apprehensive about his condition that day. Changes were taking place. Each time I looked, he seemed quiet and restful. However, as we finished lunch, I sensed a new quietness and left the table to observe him more closely. His heartbeat was still steady, but he was totally unresponsive. Perhaps She was responding to his request.

I assumed he was in a coma, although I was not sure. I called the hospice office to verify what was happening and was relieved when Jolyn answered the phone.

"Jolyn, this is Marsha. How can you tell if someone has slipped into a coma?"

"Well, they're generally unresponsive as though they are in a deep sleep. Do you think Bill is in a coma?"

"Yes, I think he is."

"Do you want someone to come over?"

"No, I don't think that's necessary. He seems peaceful and content."

"When Barb comes in, I'll ask her to stop by. Call if you need anything before then."

"Thanks."

I turned to George and confirmed that Bill was in a coma and explained how reassuring it was to be able to name what was happening. So many unfamiliar and frightening changes occurred throughout the disease process. I was relieved when I knew what was happening was "normal."

George and I talked a bit more as he explained why he couldn't stay but hated to leave. I understood and actually was grateful to be alone with Bill, although he was no longer there in the same way. Without knowing it our last conversations were shared. We'd told each other of our love for the last time. I was flooded with a tremendous sense of loss and emptiness at that moment, aware that his final hour was drawing near. I sat with him for a while, speaking what remained in my heart, hoping he was truly able to hear me. In that I relied on the medical professionals who claim hearing was the last sense to leave. There wasn't really all that much to say. Through the months of our confinement, some wonderful opportunities were taken to say it all.

After a bit, I left his bed to do some chores: dishes, laundry, and a few housekeeping tasks. It was extremely helpful to have those things to do because the time seemed endless. I felt so helpless and out of control with the changes in Bill that I welcomed being able to accomplish some things, to have a sense of control over life in some dimensions.

As I moved through the chores, I experienced panic at the prospect that he might die that day. I was all alone. There were no visitors expected. What would I do? I couldn't catch my breath. Was this normal?

There was so much that was confusing and unclear. Bill appeared peaceful in his comatose state, and I felt envious. In some ways the struggle for life was ending for him. For me the struggle to live without him was just beginning. I longed to be past whatever that was going to feel like, and I dreaded the moment it would happen. As friends became aware of his coma, they called and offered comfort and an opportunity to share some of my anxiety and sadness.

Eventually the day drew to a close, and I settled down to await the arrival of Lydia. Her presence gave me a much needed respite every night that week. She reassured me that she would watch for any changes and get me if it became necessary. I wanted very much to be with him when the final moment arrived. I slept fitfully and awoke several times to check on Bill's condition. Lydia reassured me that things were the same and encouraged me to try to sleep.

She left promptly at 6:00 a.m. and would not return until the following Monday evening. I made arrangements with friends of ours to stay Saturday night and my sister would stay on Sunday. When the hospice nurse arrived that morning, she confirmed that Bill was dying but couldn't say when the end might come. His vital signs remained strong, even though his wonderfully expressive eyes were closed and his melodic voice was quieted. Friends dropped in throughout the day but no one stayed very long. It was too painful for me, and I knew I would do better on my own. It was too difficult to interact with others. When Don and Jean arrived to spend the night, I went to bed but woke about 4:00 a.m. I went to the living room to check on Bill and knew there was a change, but I wasn't able to describe what it was. I knew he was farther along on his journey.

I didn't want to call the hospice nurse on call that early so I waited a few hours. When I talked with her, she offered to come. Once again she found his vital signs strong, and she left saying there really was no way of knowing how long he might linger. I thanked Don and Jean for their help and bid them farewell. I knew they wanted to stay longer, but I knew it was almost time and I wanted to have that time alone with him.

When Bill began the "death rattle," I knew time was closing in on us. Suddenly I felt overwhelmed with what was about to happen. I left the living room and went to the basement so I could talk to and try to settle myself. I didn't want to generate any unnecessary anxiety around Bill. The toll of this care-giving was beginning to mount. I felt frazzled, angry, impatient, and very fearful. I knew his death was near, but I feared it would not come soon enough, concerned that I might lose my own equilibrium. It helped to take time apart, away from the stress of his gurgling and the sight of his motionless body. It restored my ability to deal with it all, at least for another period of time.

CHAPTER THIRTY-NINE

The phone rang a short time later, and I realized how fragile my restoration really was. Bill's sister, Marie, announced that she was coming that afternoon and would stay until he died. I gasped at the prospect of her being present for whatever period of time remained. Marie had been a very controlling person throughout Bill's life. So many times he shared his distress after he spent time with her, which he did often as she was his only unmarried sister, and she lived with their parents until they died. Bill tried to reach out to her through the years but felt he made little progress in improving their relationship. I knew he would not want her present, for his sake or for mine.

"Marie, there's really no point. He's in a coma, as you know. I'll call as soon as anything happens."

"I'm coming this afternoon." She was almost always rude and abrupt with me. My chest felt constricted, and I experienced another wave of powerlessness. If she came, I would have to endure even greater tension and I didn't need that. I walked to Bill's bed, and as calmly as possible I explained to him. "Bill, that was Marie. She said she is coming today and plans to stay as long as necessary. I'm sure you know how difficult that would be for me. I don't know what you can do to stop her, but I really need some help right now. It will be just awful if she does come. If you can do anything, please try to help."

I walked about the house and tried to restore a bit more calm. I remembered how often she agitated him about his own personal growth and the changes she didn't like, especially his friendship with me. He avoided any confrontation with her usually, but a year earlier he addressed it with all three of his sisters. He had been reluctant to share his illness with them, expecting them to be unable to deal with it; however, the cancer diagnosis was serious and ominous. At my urging, he arranged to tell them what was happening in his body. He told me they were fairly silent initially. The news was shocking and caused great sadness. His sister Margaret asked how they could help.

"Just pray for me and try to support what Marsha and I are doing in Wisconsin. I want you to stop referring to her as 'my associate' and call her by name. She has been my good friend for many years. I depend on her and she has helped me through some difficult situations. Please use her name when you speak of her."

He was relieved when he returned after their meeting and encouraged by their change of heart toward me. They treated me much better and even included me in occasional family celebrations. By the time Bill's health deteriorated to the point of requiring hospice care, they were showered me with gratitude. They fully realized Bill would have finished his life in a nursing home had I not been there.

I knew Bill would not want Marie there during his dying moments. She had visited the day before and carried on in a very agitated manner. Other family members tried to quiet her so as to maintain the atmosphere of peace that surrounded Bill's dying process. If she were to return, that peace would be dramatically interrupted again.

Even though it was very cold that February morning, I stepped outside on the snow-covered deck and inhaled the crisp, fresh air. This had been a wonderful place for us, a place where we shared many good times. We always left here restored and renewed and able to return to whatever the work place offered. I reached down to pet Rosie. She was staying very close to me, sensing something was going on. She already missed Bill's attention. She would sit in a corner of the living room and just look at him as he lay motionless on the bed. We both were losing a great friend.

It was almost time for his medication so I returned to the living room, grateful for the warmth of the house. I hadn't realized how cold I became in those few minutes. I shivered as I walked to his bed. "Bill, I don't know what I can do for you right now. I hope you're as comfortable and pain-free as you seem. I'm here and I'll be here as long as you need me. I won't leave you alone. I love you, Bill."

I walked to the other side of the bed to administer his medication and noticed his breathing was very rapid, then shallow and intermittent, until finally he exhaled one last time. *Oh my God, he's dead.* I reached under his head and held him close to my heart, and I sobbed from the depths of my soul. He was gone forever; his life and mine changed forever.

The phone rang then and I placed his head and shoulders gently on the pillow. It was his niece, calling to say she was unable to bring Marie today. There were just too many things going on at her house; maybe tomorrow she could come. I felt Bill had taken this matter into his own hands and smiled through my tears.

"Susie, your uncle just died this minute. I'll call hospice as soon as we finish, but I know he's dead."

"Thanks be to God. Why did he struggle so long? We kept asking ourselves that question?"

"He didn't want to die, Susie. He was happier these past couple of years than he had been in a long time. He loved what we were doing at The Barn. He desperately wanted to continue what we started."

There was no response to that; I don't think she fully understood. Since she had been asked by her uncle to handle his funeral arrangements, we moved to that conversation and determined who each of us would contact with the sad news. Then we hung up.

Immediately, the phone rang again and the hospice nurse was on the other end. She was just calling to check; she had a feeling he would die soon but didn't want to alarm me unnecessarily. I told her he'd just died and she said she'd be right there. She arrived shortly, gave me a reassuring and caring hug and then moved to Bill to tend to him briefly. Then she called his physician, Chris. There was no coroner to be contacted; no ambulance siren to be endured. That was another gift of hospice.

When Chris and Kathy completed their conversation, he asked to talk with me. "Marsha, I'm so very sorry for your loss. You did such a wonderful job with him. He was so lucky to have you. I've been in awe of your commitment to him. It has been a powerful lesson for me."

"Thanks, Chris, but you were great, too. Bill had such confidence in you and trusted you throughout the entire time. I relied on you very much, too, and you never let me down." With that my tears began again, and I passed the phone to Kathy. She concluded her business with Chris and called the funeral home. When the undertaker arrived and removed Bill's body, the house echoed with tomb-like silence. Rosie and I sat in the family room, staring out the window at the now empty driveway. She was such a wonderfully sensitive dog who realized that something terrible had happened. From that day on, she never entered that house through the front door. She had seen Bill carried through it all covered up.

Kathy prepared to leave, solicitous about me for the rest of the day. Some friends who lived nearby offered to come and stay for a while and my sister, Lee was on her way. She had planned to sit with Bill through the night; as it was, we sat together without him. She suggested we return to The Barn right away, but I wanted to spend that night where he spent his last hours. I was surprised at the conflicting emotions I was feeling. The sadness was pervasive, but I also felt relieved, as though a heavy burden had been raised from my chest and shoulders. This had been a long and arduous journey, this walk to death, and I was bone and spirit weary.

CHAPTER FORTY

I sat quietly in the pew of the large church that had been Bill's last pastorate. He had requested that his funeral liturgy be celebrated there. The organ was a magnificent Hammond, purchased new during Bill's time there. I was soothed by the soft sounds and vaguely aware of the muted voices of the gathering congregation. My deep brown eyes were red and swollen from the events of the past few days, but they took in the activity taking place around the altar. Priests and servers were readying the space for the liturgy. For a moment, I recalled how much Bill had been involved in that space and I felt a wave of loss.

The vestments were white. Death was supposed to be a joyous occasion that celebrated the return of the person to God. I did not feel one bit joyful. The burning candles, floral pieces and incense being prepared to greet the casket that contained Bill was not lifting my spirits as it once had. It was not only Bill's death; so much had changed for me. The momentary comfort of the warm embraces of those gathering to celebrate, their soothing words and reassurances of concern helped, but I knew I would not ever be comfortable in a setting like this again.

I felt smaller today, more so than I knew I appeared. Generally slender, I was now quite thin. My sense of smallness today was more reflective of a deep vulnerability. I had no idea what would become of me or what I would do in the future. I hoped to continue The Barn, but I was not ready for that just now. Bill was such a vital part of my life these past twenty years. The Church, to which I had dedicated thirty of my adult years, offered me no direction or comfort.

I was very grateful for Bill's invitation to participate in planning this liturgy and for the opportunity to give this homily. It seemed totally improbable that I would be able to do it. After all, just a few short years earlier, I had been silenced. The Cardinal who delivered the final ultimatum from Rome was in attendance as were one of the local Bishops and a myriad of priests. When George finished his homily, I would be allowed to share my words.

Suddenly the organ exploded and the sounds of the opening hymn filled the entire church. The ministers gathered at the altar and walked to the entrance of the church to greet the casket and family. My eyes filled with tears once again, and I wondered whether I would even be able to speak when the time came. My body was weak and my knees shook as I stood with the rest of the congregation to await the arrival of the casket.

When it was beside me, I turned toward it and tried to still my heart's anguish. As the liturgy began, I felt myself regaining a sense of composure. I needed to do this homily; it would be very difficult. It was the last attempt Bill made to let people know how convinced he was about the need for changes in the liturgy, especially with regard to the role of women.

When George completed his homily, which included some gracious words about the man who had been his friend through all the years, he sat in his presidia's chair. I stood and began the walk down the aisle past Bill's casket. I placed my hand on it and paused a moment. *Please, Bill, help me to do this with dignity and strength.* He knew what I planned to say since I had shared it with him one of the last days he was conscious.

When I said what I planned to say, his face revealed calmness and peace and the loving look in his eyes as I began were enough to motivate me to continue. He was deeply moved by my words, reflected in the tears that began to well up as I completed what I had written so far. "Bill, there's one part I haven't written yet, but I know I will have to say something about our relationship."

He had enough energy to give a sheepish grin and added, "I suppose you will, but remember I won't be there this time." With that he reached his arms through the hospital bed and invited me to hold him, as we both sobbed.

I reached the lectern, steadied myself on its polished wooden frame and recalled briefly the exhilaration and joy I recalled from previous experiences in this same spot. I remember, too, the pain and conflict it generated, but this was a new moment and I began.

"This past summer when Bill came to the realization that the cancer that invaded his body was out of control, he talked with George and me about his wishes for his funeral and burial. Eucharist was always very significant to Bill, and he wanted his resurrection liturgy to reflect who he was and was becoming and what really had become important to him in his later years. He entrusted the privilege of trying to communicate that to George and me.

"The choice of readings came from our experiences during these last two years. When we embarked on the ministry at The Barn, we had a sense that we wanted to create an environment for persons to reclaim themselves, their true selves, recover from whatever contributed to their being less than they could be, and to recreate new ways of living, praying and relating that would nurture the best of who they were.

"As the months went on, we sensed that the Spirit who had called each of us was still in process with us and with the direction we were trying to pursue. We and the ministry were in the process of being shaped and molded. We tried as best we could to become pliable in the hands of the Potter God.

"Bill moved beyond the God of our tradition who has been exclusively celebrated as Father. He embraced a God who was Mother as well, a God who was beyond gender. Bill grew to love the God he knew as Creator, who called all living things to life, and who called all of us to be in relationship with the entire created world.

"As priest, pastor and friend, he encouraged all to believe in the gift of the Spirit present within each person. Often he failed to see how that same spirit was doing wonderful things in and through him. Only in his later years, as he began to trust that movement within him, was he able to move beyond expectations of institutional Church family and role to become free. As a result, Bill chose not to return to parish ministry when he completed his sabbatical. There was no life for him there any more and his wonderful Jesuit spiritual director encouraged him to go where he found life.

"He did that and people wondered, questioned and criticized him. We don't always understand or want to see another become free. We like to keep them the way we have always seen them. Bill continued to trust the movement of the Spirit within him and was more and more able to let go of all that kept him fettered and unfree.

"Bill was so like Jesus, who moved beyond structural and cultural limitations to encourage women and men to develop their gifts and talents for leadership and service. He invited girls as well as boys to serve at the altar. He was open and responsive to the gifts of the Spirit wherever they were manifest. For that, like Jesus, he was often criticized.

"Bill was truly priest, but he did not cling to priesthood as a mark of status or importance. He emptied himself of the trappings sometimes associated with that role and became truly priest. He served well, even in his own illness. He ministered to other cancer patients with whom he shared his five-day-a-week rides to and from radiation. I commented to him one day, 'Bill, you are always a priest but now you are freer of priesthood.' 'That's a good way to put it,' he said.

"Bill knew his ability to serve and function was enhanced by his ability to enter into loving relationships. In our friendship, each of us found life, energy and love which enabled us to be for others. When we heard comments about our ministry at The Barn, we were puzzled. 'They're only doing that because they love each other.' Isn't love the driving force in ministry? Or is love a deterrent to ministry? Our experience and our history is testimony to the fact that our love for each other, for God and for others was the impelling energy of our ministry.

"Bill didn't want to die. He struggled with the onset of death. In many ways, he felt he had just begun to live. He did some wonderful things in his life and his marvelous spirit will continue to manifest itself in those of us who had the privilege of knowing him. We have lost a great person and we will grieve for a long time."

When I completed the homily, I returned to my pew and I thanked Bill for his help as I touched the casket once more. When I reached my seat, I suddenly felt exhausted and totally depleted, but I was so grateful to have this opportunity to bid farewell to Bill. I knew I was also saying good-bye to the institution as well. It is finished.

Following the liturgy I attended the reception in the parish hall, which was buzzing with all kinds of talk and laughter. I was dazed and went through the motions of listening to the words of comfort, consolation, condolences, and praise for my courageous talk. There were many priests present, most of whom I knew. None of them approached me, except for the Bishop who came to me and said, "Well, Marsha, now what?"

I didn't bother to respond. I doubted that he was really interested in my next steps, and truth be told, I didn't even know myself what was next. Bill and I had talked about my future one day.

"Marsha, do you think you can continue The Barn alone?" he'd asked.

"I'll give it my best, but it will be difficult without you. Do you think I can do it alone?"

"Absolutely!"

I would certainly give it my best effort but I knew I needed some time to recover and grieve the loss of Bill and the loss of the Church. I left the reception to pick up Rosie from my friends' house and returned in time to enter the funeral procession to the cemetery, for the final ritual before placing his casket in the ground. When that was completed, I walked with heaviness of spirit to my car, and Rosie and I set off for Wisconsin. It was a very lonely trip and I was so exhausted when I arrived at The Barn that I fell into a deep sleep. Tomorrow would be time enough to think about what the future held.

EPILOGUE

I did, in fact, continue the spiritual ministry at The Barn. I was deeply grieved at Bill's loss and I felt at times that the loneliness would overwhelm me. I sought grief counseling in a local group to help me through some of the most difficult periods. I tried to follow the program we had established, with the exception of Sunday Eucharist. While some of the group was enthusiastic and responsive to the possibility of my being the celebrant, there was strong opposition from others. The latter discontinued their participation in any of The Barn activities.

That was an extremely distressing experience. My energies were at an all-time low, and I knew I could not muster the personal resources I needed to sustain myself through the inevitable conflict that would ensue if I were to continue the Sunday liturgy. I felt as though I was once again thrust into the restrictiveness of the institution.

Activities that required the presence of an ordained minister were discontinued. The opportunity for centering prayer and retreats for individuals and small groups continued at The Barn.

Additional programs in spirituality were offered and held in a larger facility closer to town. The Barn continued to serve as my home for several years until a new phase of my journey began.

~END~